COUNTERPOINTS

COUNTERPOINTS

The Dynamics of Believing Today

Douglas Alan Walrath

The Pilgrim Press

New York

Copyright © 1991 by The Pilgrim Press

All rights reserved. Except for brief quotations used in critical articles or reviews, no part of this book may be reproduced, stored in a retrieval system, or transmitted by any means without the prior written permission of the publisher.

Scripture quotations are from the New Revised Standard Version Bible, copyright 1989, Division of Christian Education of the National Council of the Churches of Christ in the United States of America, and are used by permission.

Book design by Patricia Kellis.

Cover design by Jim Gerhard.

Walrath, Douglas Alan, 1933–
      Counterpoints : the dynamics of believing today / Douglas Alan Walrath.
          p.
      Includes bibliographical references.
      ISBN 0-8298-0892-2 (alk. paper)
      1. Faith. 2. Belief and doubt. 3. Thought and thinking.
      4. Experience (Religion)   I. Title.
      BV4637.W32 1991
      231'.042 – dc20   91-7213
                                                                CIP

This book is printed on acid-free, recycled paper.

Printed in the United States of America.

10 9 8 7 6 5 4 3 2 1

The Pilgrim Press, 475 Riverside Drive, New York, NY 10115

CONTENTS

In memory of

Hugh Baillie MacLean
Scholar, teacher, mentor, and friend

PREFACE

I often hear Christians lamenting the lack of "spiritual progress" in recent times. Within Western culture, it does seem that there has not been much spiritual progress in the last two centuries. Most of the significant advances in thinking have appeared in the sciences, which, admittedly, have engaged the attention of many of the most competent among us. Few of us know more about God than our great grandparents did, while most of us understand many of the dynamics of human functioning and the workings of the natural order more accurately than most of our forebears did.

It often surprises me to see how little this improved understanding of human functioning and the natural order affects the way most of us approach believing. Many of us seem to maintain a wall between our spiritual development and the rest of our thinking. In doing so we are clearly products of our time. The church responded almost immediately to the emerging scientific thinking of the nineteenth and twentieth centuries by walling itself off. In the last 150 years, many, if not most, Christians have functioned within a spiritually segregated mindset.[1]

Many of us have accepted the cultural pattern and internalized this barrier between thinking about spiritual or theological matters, that is, believing, and thinking about everything else. We maintain our believing not by subjecting it to critical challenges that could hone it and strengthen it but by giving it privileged status. We refuse to think critically about our believing. A spiritual protectiveness, which most of us take for granted, is built into Western culture. Custom protects our spiritual life from challenging encounters. We tiptoe around our believing—and expect others to do the same.

I wrote this book for those who want to break down the barrier between thinking and believing. I wrote it for those of us who are convinced that faithful believing must include critical thinking. I wrote it for those of us who feel called to be critical believers.

I think the cleavage between believing and thinking that has marked our culture has impeded the development of both. We have not, for example, developed ways of believing that take into account the psychological and cultural bias that shapes all human believing, past and present, our own included. Rather than developing approaches that subject our believing to critical scrutiny that could challenge and strengthen it, we protect it— and live on with biases that lead to serious, even tragic, consequences for ourselves and others. Many of us are defensive about our beliefs because we are afraid that our believing may be fragile and naive.

Often our fears are justified. To be sound our believing does need to be honed and strengthened by critical thinking. Simple believing is not necessarily enviable.

My experience and research suggest that finding solid approaches to believing is a common challenge that thinking believers face today. Four years ago, after a decade of research and reflection, I wrote *Frameworks: Patterns of Living and Believing Today*. In this book I describe the difficulties contemporary Christian believers face, as well as some of the different approaches Christians now take to living and believing. The next year I wrote *Options: How to Develop and Share Christian Faith Today*. In this book I offer some suggestions to those who want to share Christian faith with others. The present book, *Counterpoints: The Dynamics of Believing Today*, which appears third in this trilogy, is actually out of order. Only after *Options* appeared did I realize I took too much for granted when I wrote it. It should have appeared third, after *Counterpoints;* those who choose to read all three books will find it most helpful to read *Counterpoints* second and *Options* third.

I think that spiritual formation will be the major concern of the church during the next decade. And for good reason: many of us are facing a crisis of believing. Western culture no longer honors compartmentalized believing. The barrier between believing and thinking is down. Challengers no longer tiptoe around believing Christians. If we choose to think and want our believing to survive, we will have to become competent believers.

As a result of the more critical atmosphere, attributes of God that Christians have long taken for granted are no longer automatically believable or acceptable to us. For example, we do not simply accept the fact that God is present in all of life if God's presence is not apparent to us—in fact, when much of the evidence we observe seems to argue to the contrary. Nor are we willing to accept the role that women are assigned in scripture as divinely ordaining them forever to second-class status when critical perspectives indicate that the subservient roles in which they are cast are simply an accident of culture. And so on.

I hope *Counterpoints* will provide critical believers with helpful tools. As the chapter titles indicate, I am convinced that the human dynamics of believing require counterpoints. Thus, the inspiration we perceive within requires the counterpoint of inspiration others perceive that we do not; our certainty needs the counterpoint of doubt to confront us with questions lest we be led astray by our certainty.

Throughout *Counterpoints* I distinguish between believing and faith. Believing I define as a human activity. Like thinking and perceiving it is subject to all our human foibles and limits. Faith I define, in line with most Christian theologians, as a gift of God. Believing is something we develop; faith is possible only because God gives it to us. Not everyone distinguishes between these two words as I do; but the arguments of the book will be more understandable to those who are aware of the distinction I make between believing and faith.

Many people help to make a book possible. Over the last several years, students and faculty at Bangor Theological Seminary, where I teach, have given me the benefit of their critical thinking. Among others, I am grateful to David Dodge, former student, now colleague in ministry, who encouraged me to believe it would be helpful to share my approach to scripture with others. Ann Johnston, professor of Hebrew scriptures at Bangor, was particularly helpful in my attempt to understand Old Testament culture and to render Hebrew texts faithfully.

Sherry, my wife, will again recognize how much I gain from her insights. Page after page reflects suggestions she has given me during challenging conversations. Her spiritual honesty exemplifies critical believing.

This book is dedicated to the memory of Hugh Baillie MacLean, who many years ago opened the scriptures to me. By helping me see biblical characters as human beings, being godly became a possibility for me, not simply a concept. "Dr. Mac." died an untimely death, much too soon, but not before he showed me I didn't have to stop thinking to be a faithful believer.

COUNTERPOINTS

CHAPTER ONE

Honoring the Human Limits of Believing

It's a typical day for the church executive; he is on an airplane traveling to a meeting. After the flight attendant removes his meal tray, he begins to study the faces of those around him. He wonders what they believe and whether they participate in any church. As someone who carries major responsibility for the evangelism program of his denomination he is concerned about the image the church conveys in American society, especially among those who are not involved in it. Often when he travels he finds himself seated next to people who are not Christians and who do not participate in any church. Whenever he meets such persons he asks them to share their opinions of Christians and the church.

The young woman seated next to him today is bright, articulate, obviously well educated. She appears to be in her late thirties. Their conversation begins effortlessly; she is friendly and easy to talk with. After they have exchanged only a few sentences, she asks a surprising question. Pointing to the small cross in his coat lapel, she asks, "What is that?"

"That's a cross!" he replies, assuming that she is having difficulty seeing it without her glasses.

"A cross?" she responds. "Does that have some significance?"

The Disestablishment of Protestant Beliefs

When I share this story at gatherings of church members, it strikes most of them as unbelievable. "Everyone knows what 'the Cross' signifies," they protest.

While they are aware that many people today do not participate in any church, it strikes them as preposterous that a well-educated adult American would ask such a seemingly naive question.

While the degree of her unawareness may be unusual, the woman on the airplane is in fact quite typical. The person next to us at the neighborhood association meeting, the grocery store, the office, the swimming pool, or on the airplane is very likely not a church participant or even a Christian believer. And, as some younger adult members of a congregation in a suburb south of Boston discovered, that person may have difficulty understanding why any mature, urbane, thinking adult would be active in a church. "Suburban life today is much different from what it was in our parents' time," they told me. "We have to explain to our neighbors why we *do* go to church, not why we don't."

Most of us are aware that many people whose social position would have naturally included church activity in a former time now stand apart from the church. In the 1985 book *Habits of the Heart: Individualism and Commitment in American Life*, Robert Bellah and his coauthors describe the large number of Americans who embrace individualism but refuse to participate actively in the basic institutions of society.[1] Many Americans are now unwilling to commit themselves to the political, social, and religious organizations that enable our society to function. They want to be free to "do their own thing" without accepting responsibility for the workings of society as a whole. Two years after *Habits of the Heart* appeared, *American Mainline Religion: Its Changing Shape and Future* was published. In this book Wade Clark Roof and William McKinney trace in detail the exodus of educated, middle-class Americans from the church during the last three decades.[2] Their research reveals a new "up-and-out" pattern among church dropouts during this period. Americans who in a former time would have moved into a higher-status church when they achieved more years of formal education than their parents had, or who were able to secure a higher-status job or to improve themselves economically, now moved out when they moved up. During the 1960s, 1970s, and 1980s, they moved out of church activity altogether when they moved up educationally, occupationally, or economically.

In *The Restructuring of American Religion: Society and Faith Since World War II* Robert Wuthnow describes the end result of the shifts Roof and McKinney trace.[3] The American religious landscape is now more complex. The emergence of a variety of religious groups complicates the traditional Protestant, Catholic or Jew pattern of affiliation described in 1955 by Will Herberg.[4] Diversity has even increased within the Christian churches with the growth of such varied movements as Christian feminism and the new evangelicalism. These groups elicit loyalties that cut across the old denominational lines. They probably claim the allegiance of more persons than remain in all the old, middle-class churches combined.

As helpful as they are, I think the *organizational* focus of these recent studies limits their usefulness. They are largely concerned with changing patterns of participation in organized religious bodies. They trace the waning commitment of middle-class people, especially educated middle-class people, to church activity during the 1960s, 1970s, and 1980s.[5] They describe the declining influence of the mainline church. Their argument that the dominant role traditionally played by mainline, Protestant churches in rural America, city neighborhoods, and more recently in suburbia is now largely a matter of history is convincing. But identifying the reasons for this decline is more difficult. It is far easier to note the head count in various denominations from year to year than it is to fathom what is going on inside the heads of those of us who would have been active Presbyterians or Episcopalians in a former time, but who have chosen not to be in this time.

When I review the history of the last four decades, it seems clear to me that the mainstream *culture* of America has experienced fundamental changes, and that changes in church participation reflect these more fundamental cultural changes. I do not think that popular, simple explanations can account for the continuing alienation of so many mainstream Americans from the mainline churches. Such widespread alienation is more than simply the result of their disappointment with the churches' stance during the social revolution of the 1960s and 1970s, for example. In his book *The End of the American Future*,[6] Peter Schrag describes the pervasive social and cultural changes that occurred during the 1960s and 1970s and then argues that transformations brought about by these changes will be with us *permanently*. American life now and in the years to come will include ways of living and believing that are quite different from the normative ways of living and believing that mainstream Americans had assumed would always dominate our culture. Many mainstream Americans no longer participate in church the way their forebears did in the past because they no longer *believe* the way their forebears did.

Schrag's focus on our changing beliefs is an important shift. In our continuing research among people who currently do not participate in any church, my wife, Sherry, and I have discovered that most of them are quite clear both about what they believe and why they are not active in any church. Some describe difficult relationships with church members or clergy as contributing to their alienation from church. But nearly all of them, whether they are church dropouts or persons who have never been active in a church, offer the same explanation as the major cause of their lack of church participation. Most clergy and church members with whom they are familiar seem unable or unwilling to address their difficulty with (or objections to) what they think Christians *believe*. Church members want them to come (back) to church, but they don't seem to know how to talk with them about believing.[7]

Those who study the declining influence of mainline Protestant churches commonly use the term disestablish-

ment to describe these churches' loss of their dominant role in society.[8] While it has received relatively little
notice from the researchers, I think many Americans
have experienced a theological disestablishment along
with this institutional displacement. Many of us are
theologically as well as organizationally disconnected from
the old mainline churches. Not only is the traditional
church no longer the integrating center of our lives, the
approach that most mainline church members have typi-
cally taken to believing is not the way we approach
believing. The way many of us learned that Christians
should approach believing (and the way many do) is fun-
damentally at odds with the way we approach believing.

Many Americans are no longer willing to subordinate
their believing to the authority of a church. This unwill-
ingness is rooted in a cultural disestablishment that par-
alleled and, I think, largely facilitated the institutional
disestablishment of the mainline church. During the
first three quarters of this century the mainstream culture that supported traditional approaches to believing
was disestablished.[9] As the mainline church was the
social center of the old culture, so what most people
perceived as mainline beliefs formed its theological
center. As I suggested in *Frameworks*,[10] during the establishment era, some of us wrestled with issues of believing. But when we did, we did so in an establishment
manner. Most of us struggled not to ascertain what we
believed but to accept what we assumed we were sup-
posed to believe. When our experience disagreed with
established beliefs, we redefined our experience to make
it fit established theological norms, or we assumed that
at some future time we would be able to redefine our
experience to fit the norms. In any event, we assumed
that the problem was not the church's theology but what
we believed. We had faith in the faith of the church.

Except among very conservative and fundamentalist
Christians, such a normative and submissive approach
to believing is now much less common. Normative thinking per se has become disestablished in American cul-

ture. Now many people assume they have the right and competence to do their own believing. They approach believing much more critically than most people did in the past. They do not assume that what they believe must conform to some church-mandated body of beliefs. And something much deeper than rebelliousness is at the root of this refusal.

Contemporary Believers

I first became aware of the depth of the shift away from normative thinking thirty years ago when I read *New Pathways in Science* by the British physicist Sir Arthur Eddington.[11]   None of my courses in seminary included the study of twentieth-century physics.   The study of theology did not include references to contemporary physics or economics or psychology or any other science for that matter.   My teachers evidently thought a familiarity with these disciplines was not essential for someone intent upon becoming a pastor.   Like most theological students of that time, I learned theology in relative isolation from current thinking in the natural and behavioral sciences.

Eddington's book made the first breach in the walls around my compartmentalized theology, and the insights that I encountered over the next two years completely knocked down the fortifications that surrounded my normative approach to believing. In the first chapter of *New Pathways in Science*, Eddington describes the ways every observation is affected by the presence of the observer. He suggests that completely objective perceptions are impossible. There is no way that we humans can gain an absolutely accurate picture of anything or anyone. Even our most accurate perceptions are biased. I wondered: How could our perceptions of God be unbiased, if we had biased perceptions of everything else?

During the months that followed, as I became more familiar with contemporary physics, my old approach to believing was severely challenged. I wrestled not only with the implications of Einstein's relativity, I felt the impact of the world as envisioned by W.K. Heisenberg. In his model of the creation, Newton's balanced, predictable, ordered reality gives way to a world of "indeterminacy," where particles move at random, and no one knows for sure how it all holds together. Perhaps we perceive a balance in the natural "order" only because, as statisticians suggest, the "errors cancel"?

I moved from physics to psychology and anthropology. The introductory psychology I studied as a college undergraduate had been largely behaviorism-oriented ("ratiology" was the name students gave it). Now I went on to consider Freud and Carl Jung in some depth. I was struck especially by Freud's view of the role of the unconscious in shaping what we feel and believe. I became aware of the extent to which my own and others' believing and acting are shaped by forces of which we are largely unaware. Jung introduced me to the pervasive role of myth in human believing. From Jung I learned how humans in every culture have constructed myths to help them interpret and relate to the unexplainable and mysterious.

So it went as I acted on the advice of a respected mentor and caught up with current thinking in a variety of disciplines instead of pursuing more graduate study in theology. "You already know how to learn," he said to me. "Why don't you just do it? And don't just consider theological material; read science and literature. Learn about the world in which people must do their believing." Now, as I was learning about that world, I struggled with my growing awareness of the essential relativity and ambiguity that attend all human perceiving and thinking—including believing. What I lost as my perspective widened was not simply the authority of some norms; the loss was deeper than that. I lost confidence in the normative approach. I doubted that anyone, however inspired, could perceive with absolute accuracy. And I doubted that anyone has ever perceived anything, including God, with absolute accuracy.

Looking back, I now realize why I had difficulty com-
municating what I was experiencing to most of the people
in my rural congregation. They were kind but puzzled by
the references in my sermons to the issues with which I
was struggling.   Their puzzlement is understandable to
me now; few of them were reading the books I was
reading. They were still firmly rooted in the old culture.
Most of them had heard of Einstein, but functionally
they were Newtonians.   Even when the world around
them didn't seem orderly or purposeful, they assumed it
is.   They saw the emerging social and cultural revolu-
tions of the time as only temporary diversions that would
soon pass as "things got back to normal."   They had
similar feelings about challenges to traditional ways of
believing. They could have had difficulty with some of the
theological norms they accepted, such as "the Bible is
without error," because they knew the Bible envisions a
flat world and contains contradictory stories, for example, two different versions of the Creation.   But they
chose not to examine such contradictions critically because they had more faith in the church and what the
church believed than they did in themselves and what
they perceived.   To be honest, I think they realized that
the place of the church, their church, in American society was being threatened.   They wanted to protect the
church's central influence, and to that end they chose
not to experience the dissonance between traditional and
contemporary ways of believing.   They were well aware
that some of those who took a contemporary approach
seriously took the church less seriously.

The difficulty that more and more church members,
especially younger members, were having with the traditional, normative approach to believing rarely drew the
attention of mainline clergy and other church leaders
during those years. The social revolution that began in
the 1960s engaged nearly all their energy during that
decade and the next. Perhaps the social revolution ab-
sorbed so much attention because it challenged the

churches from within as well as from without. College students were in the vanguard of the struggle for social justice. The cultural privileges and affluence enjoyed by middle-class families enabled a large number of children from these families to attend college. When college students moved into the center of the battle for social justice, mainline church members reading the morning paper or watching the news on TV saw their own children challenging their own church to give up its traditional support of the establishment culture to become a critic of that culture. The ensuing intergenerational conflict over the church's appropriate role in society dominated the church's agenda for many years.

The debate over the church's proper response to social justice concerns helped to disengage a large number of mainstream Americans, especially younger mainstream Americans, from the church. It may even have precipitated the exodus of many. But it was not the primary cause of their continuing alienation from the mainline church. The critical approach to thinking and believing that I discovered in my catch-up study of the sciences became the operational approach that most educated people adopted by the 1960s. That new approach threw them out of culture with the mainline church and the old American mainstream. This cultural alienation was and is at the root of their continuing alienation from the church.

The "radical" thinking I encountered in physics and psychology during the late 1950s now seems like common sense to many of us. A later generation's willingness to accept ideas that a previous generation viewed as radical is actually a common occurrence. The working assumptions of a few in one generation often become the working assumptions of many in the next. Many of the scientific perspectives that challenged my thinking and believing in the 1950s are now the operating assumptions of many, if not most, educated adults. These perspectives, which encourage critical thinking in approaching *any* subject, including religion, were held by only an educated elite in the first half of this century. Now they have become the perspectives of a much larger proportion of our society, for at least two reasons. First, beginning with the years immediately after World War II, many more Americans went on to college, where they were encouraged and equipped to think critically. Second, geographical mobility increased. Many more people moved away from their roots. Living far away from home, they lost the feelings of accountability and sense of obligation to tradition that go with living one's entire life in the same community, within eyesight of one's parents and extended family. Those who live beyond the scrutinizing eyes of neighbors and family are less likely to feel obligated to maintain traditional lifestyles and ways of thinking.

As a result of the profound cultural and social changes during the past half century, many more people in our society are now equipped to think critically and feel free to do so. They approach believing from the same critical perspective as they approach all of life. These critical believers now form the core of what was once the American mainstream.

Believers who are committed to this critical approach are not limited to those who have left the church. Though they might not label themselves as "critical believers," during nearly two decades of conversations with church members about their approach to believing, I have found a large number of persons who continue as members of mainline churches but who actually function as critical believers. Their approach to believing is similar to that of people who do not participate in any church, but who would have been active in a mainline church during the pre-1960s, establishment era.[12] Whether they are active in the church or nonparticipants, the church is disestablished for both groups. They are not willing to give any church absolute authority over their believing.

The Inescapable Humanity of Believing

Critical believers prefer the diversity that contemporary society encourages to the normative believing that was expected in the old, establishment culture. But their support of the pluralism that marks American society is not based on some fuzzy notion of tolerance or a belief that norms are unnecessary. It stems from a profound awareness of human limits, an awareness supported by insights into the nature of human beings that have emerged during the past hundred years and that many of us now accept as valid. On the basis of these insights, critical believers think an open, critical approach to believing is essential.

Two interrelated assumptions govern the critical believers' approach. They assume (1) that all our mental images, including our pictures of God, are models we construct based on less than perfect perceptions of what really exists, and (2) that we intentionally or unwittingly bias whatever we perceive in order to maintain our models.

Constructed Versions of Reality

According to the first assumption, everyone's version of reality is a *constructed* version. Each of us is a perceiver who interprets and then builds a mental model. Whenever we perceive, we interpret in the process of perceiving. We make sense out of what we perceive by selecting certain perceptions that seem significant to us and ignoring others. We then put these selected perceptions together in ways that seem logical to us. The result is a model based on what we have chosen and assembled. Together our models represent our picture of what is. One person's model is more or less accurate than another person's model, but neither one person's model nor anyone else's is a completely accurate representation of actuality. No human model represents exactly what truly exists.[13]

If this assumption about the process of perceiving is accurate, it has profound implications for the process of believing. Unless by some means we cease being human perceivers when God communicates with us, we interpret whatever God reveals to us in the process of perceiving it. We construct mental models utilizing the perceptions that seem significant to us. Our ability to perceive what God reveals is subject to the same human limitations as our ability to perceive anything else.

If we accept the reality of these inherent limitations of human believing, the widespread disagreement among Christians about what God is like and what God wants humans to be should no longer surprise us. Each one's believing is subject to the limits of his or her perceiving. Humans construct different models based on their differing perceptions. To believe, as some Christians do, that God's revelation overcomes our human perceptual limits seems contrary to common experience (and, as I shall propose in the next chapter, can be dangerous). We Christians *do* disagree about what God is like and about what God wants us to be. We *do* perceive God differently. We *do* believe differently.

Even what we learn about God from scripture is affected by our ability to perceive. Personally, I believe that scripture reveals what God is like. But scripture presents a very complex picture of God. It presents God as loving, considerate, patient, rigid, harsh, even as one who seeks vengeance.[14] When we consider such conflicting attributes, how do we know what God is like?

I think we decide. As we weigh the various descriptions of God's nature and activity in scripture, certain images impress us. We choose among these impressions and construct a model that seems to us to reflect what God is like. We perceive God as revealed in scripture in terms of a model we construct. Even those of us who believe that faith is possible only because God chooses to speak and act must come to terms with the fact that we too perceive God's word and activity as human believers.

Even when we pray for God's guidance, we receive that guidance through the limits of our humanity.

Biased Believing

Our believing is not only limited and biased by the models we construct; it is biased by our efforts to maintain these models. According to the second core assumption, once our beliefs are in place, we perceive selectively to reinforce them. We interact with the world and other people in ways designed to keep our beliefs intact. The process can be very subtle and also insidious. When we ask questions, the language we use to frame the questions, as well as others' perceptions of what we can understand, or what answers we are looking for, shape the answers we receive. The models of reality we construct and hold to are biased both by what we are looking for and by what others think we are looking for or can handle or appreciate.

For example, most of us recognize that women are viewed differently in cultures dominated by men and in cultures where men and women exert equal influence. What we may not recognize is that women may be viewed differently in male-dominated cultures not only because men view them differently but because *they view themselves differently* and tend to behave differently as a result. For example, some women who don't want to defer to men may continue to do so because they have accepted a culturally based, theological perspective that leads them to believe God wants them to defer to men. Men who see women defer may then conclude that women's deference is evidence that God intended them to defer to men. In such situations both men and women function to maintain the perceptual models they have built. Men continue to dominate women and women continue to defer to men, each telling the others and themselves that in doing so they are living as God intended.

Insofar as there is no such human reality as an unbiased perception, there is no such human reality as unbiased believing. The revelation we receive, like every other perception, is *always* subject to our interpretation. Faith depends on what God chooses to reveal; our faith is shaped by what we choose to believe, as suggested by the following diagram:

What we believe may reflect quite accurately what God reveals to us. But it is never more than "quite" accurately; inevitably, we always, to some extent, misperceive what God reveals. While, as St. Paul suggests, we may perceive with complete accuracy in some future life to come, our vision in this life is limited; our perceptions are only dim reflections of what actually exists (1 Cor. 13:12). In this life, we are inescapably human believers.

Honoring the Limits of Believing

The central theme of this book is my conviction that every point of our believing requires a counterpoint to counteract the partiality and bias that are inherent in all human believing. As perceivers, as believers, we never overcome the limits of our own believing. We are much more likely to discover sound faith when we understand

and honor these limits. When we recognize that even our most accurate pictures of God and the world are biased models, at best only "dim reflections" of what actually exists, we are more likely to examine our beliefs critically. We are also more likely to examine the beliefs of others critically, including the traditions that come to us out of the past. Once we understand the process of believing, a critical approach to believing that honors the human limits of believing seems not only desirable but essential.

What might be involved in such a critical approach? Above all, I think it is important to recognize that our ability to believe develops. To do so we need to distinguish between faith and believing. About a decade ago James Fowler's *Stages of Faith*[15] was published. After I read this book, I placed it in the psychology section of my personal library, not the theology section. I think the title is unfortunately misleading. It invites conflict with Christian theologians who have long maintained (and rightly so, I believe) that faith is a gift of God. We can know and trust God only because God graciously enters our world and our lives. The theologians are right: there is an important distinction between being a believer and being a faithful believer.

I think Fowler and some others in the misnamed field of "faith development" are not as clear about the distinction between faith and believing as they need to be. Fowler does *not* describe "faith development" in *Stages of Faith*; he traces the normal expanding ability of humans to believe. Drawing primarily on developmental psychologists such as Jean Piaget and psycho-social developmentalists such as Erik Erickson, Fowler describes how our ability to believe develops and changes as we pass through various stages of human life. He shows how the way we function as believers at each stage reflects our psychological development.

It seems to me that developmental psychology can offer useful insights into the development of our human ability to believe. If our development is typical, the *way* we believe at each developmental stage will reflect characteristics that are typical of persons at this stage of development. Young children, for example, usually employ fixed, literal, concrete concepts in their believing. Adolescents usually explore what they believe from a variety of perspectives, often idealistically, and are thus constantly questioning themselves. According to Fowler, not only *is* the way we approach believing when we are ten years old different from our approach when we are fifty years old, it *should be* different. Since we are forty years older at fifty, our psychological and intellectual abilities should be more developed. If we still believe (functionally) like ten-year-olds when we are fifty, then we may be developmentally disabled. Or, we may be retaining cultural norms that impede our development.

Psychological theory that relates the ability to believe to human development also suggests that the way we believe when we are healthy is different from the way we believe when we are not. If we are healthy, interdependent persons, we will approach believing differently from the way we would if we were unhealthy, co-dependent persons. If we are so dependent on our church that we must include only the stated beliefs of our church in our believing, or if we live a self-destructive life because we are unable to challenge the beliefs imposed on us by an abusive parent, we are unhealthy believers. We can be abnormal believers as well as immature believers, to employ psychological categories. We may distort what God reveals so much that our models of what God wants for us or others encourage us to behave in ways that are hazardous to ourselves or others.

Finally, psycho-social theory suggests that our particular social position and culture shape our believing. Whether we are middle class or working class, female or male, black or Asian or white or Native American; whether we are an immigrant or a sixth-generation American, a Southerner or a New Englander, a Presbyterian or a Pentecostal, individually or in combination, shapes our approach to believing.

I often observe the close relationship between development and believing in my own children and grandchildren. When my eight-year-old granddaughter talked about her understanding of God during a recent visit, she made plain to me that she pictures God in very concrete terms. She sees God as the one who made the world in a manner roughly similar to the Creation stories in the book of Genesis. She described God to me using very human images as a powerful Person who is above, over, and present in the world in very graphic terms.

I do not picture God in many of the ways my granddaughter does. But it would be very inappropriate for me to challenge her ways of believing at this stage of her development. The images of God she currently holds are suitable for someone who is eight. However, her models of God are less than adequate for someone who is a normal fifty-year-old. To maintain that the Creation as portrayed in the book of Genesis is scientifically accurate requires something other than faith for a normal fifty-year-old; it requires self-deception. The first Genesis story of Creation envisions the earth as flat. It envisions the sun moving across the sky. To make our faith in God's creation of the world dependent on believing that the earth is flat or that the sun moves around the earth rather than the earth revolving on its axis, when we know from all the available evidence that the earth is not flat and that days and nights result from the earth's revolving, in the end weakens rather than strengthens our faith. Faith that depends on denying what we perceive (or could perceive) is not only immature; it can be hazardous to the believer and to others. The next chapter will explore in detail the need and benefits of trusting both the inspiration we perceive *and* the inspiration others perceive.

An approach to believing that makes possible faith in an eight-year-old may impede or distort faith in a fifty-year-old. To recognize that the creation is different and more complex than people realized when Genesis was written is to recognize that those who wrote the scripture were as human as we are. They worked within their perceptual models the same way we do. They believed in the same way we do. They had great faith, but they conceived of God and God's relationship to them and to the world in terms of the models available to them. They were people of faith, but at the same time they were also human believers.

When we accept the fact that we are human believers, and that normally our approach to believing should develop, we are more likely to encourage that development. To be an adult believer is to accept responsibility for our own believing. I think many Christians maintain childish attitudes in their relationship with God. There is a difference between being a childlike believer and a childish believer. In the scriptural incident[16] when Jesus holds up a child as an example to the disciples, he exhorts them (and us) to be childlike believers, to approach believing with the openness and freshness of children.

Such a fresh and open approach to believing encourages us to let our believing develop and to aid that development. We recognize that whatever we believe we decided to believe. We accept the fact that all our beliefs are models based on either our decisions or someone else's decisions to accept certain perceptions as valid. We realize that sound faith depends not only on the revealing activity of God; it depends on our willingness to hold to even the best of our beliefs tentatively.

Letting go of familiar beliefs is rarely easy. We become dependent on our beliefs. To keep them we need to protect them. Many of us are tempted to hallow past believers, to imagine that they were on the whole better believers than we can be. We become attached to old, familiar models of God and godliness. The old songs are seductive: "Give me the old time religion. . . . It was good enough for grandma; it's good enough for me." But the task of every grandchild is to examine whether what was good enough in grandma's (or grandpa's) believing is still "good enough for me."

The challenge to sort out the elements in our faith that accurately reflect God from those that reflect outmoded beliefs we need to relinquish is never ending and essential. People in each generation take convincing models as the equivalent of what exists. For a long time most people thought the physical world was actually like Newton's model, that it was governed by rigid laws. In much the same way previous generations thought the creation resembled Ptolemy's model, in which the sun revolves around the earth. When faced with new perspectives, they found it no easier to let go of comfortable and familiar models than we do. History presents a pathetic picture of the seventeenth-century bishops forcing Galileo to deny his perception that the revolving-earth model of Copernicus is more accurate than the sun-around-the-earth model of Ptolemy. Their point was that the sun must rise and fall because that is the picture of creation that Genesis presents. Galileo's point was that what is, is, regardless of whether we perceive it accurately. Tradition has it that he made his point in a comment under his breath after they had forced him to deny what he perceived. It went something like, "It doesn't matter what I say; the world is as it is."

Theological perceptions are like any other perceptions. A theologian such as Jurgen Moltmann is subject to the same human limits as a psychologist such as Carl Jung or a physicist such as Marie Curie. Each is a perceiver and a model builder. God is no more captured in Moltmann's theology than the human psyche is in Jung's psychology.

Even the most gifted and the most competent humans never capture more than an approximation. A theology is like a painting. The world does not look like Renoir's paintings or Margaret Bourke White's photographs. But when we look at Renoir's paintings or White's photographs, we are challenged to see the world his way or to look at it from her angle. In the same way when we read Rosemary Radford Ruether's theology, we are challenged to see God from her angle. Her angle is not mine, and that challenge, to see God from her angle, is valuable and, perhaps, even essential to my discovering sound faith.

Even the most respected believers of the past should not be exempt from our critical believing. St. Paul, who stands with the greatest and most insightful believers, gives us the inspired news he received from God that we are justified by grace, not works, that Christ has earned on our behalf the atonement with God that we could never earn. Paul also tells us that women should keep their heads covered and their mouths shut in church, that wives should be subject to their husbands, that slaves should obey their masters, and that all of us should submit ourselves to whatever ruler is in charge, even when that ruler seems abusive. Inspired as he is in the matter of our justification, Paul seems less inspired than some believers today in his views of women, slavery, and rulers. As will be explored more fully in the next chapter, even the believing of those who wrote the scripture is human believing. Even Paul's believing needs to be challenged by critical believers. I believe we will more likely be faithful today if, rather than having Paul's views, we heed Rosemary Ruether's perceptions of the role of women in the church and Rosa Parks's perception of the places black people can occupy on a bus and Desmond Tutu's perception of the way we should respond to abusive rulers.

If the insights we have gained into human believing are sound, then we need to look critically not only at our own believing but at the beliefs of others. We need to evaluate critically what those around us believe and what those who have preceded us believed. On the whole, humans in the past have never been *able* to believe better than we can today. Some past cultures may have been more supportive of those seeking to be faithful believers, and some individual believers may have been unusally faithful people. But to attribute some kind of superhuman capability to others, including those who wrote the scriptures, is to do them and ourselves a disservice. The dynamics of human functioning are the dynamics that shape believing. To be faithful we need to trust God and to honor the limits of our believing.

CHAPTER 2

Seeking Inspiration Within and Beyond Our Experience

The late summer afternoon brings a violent thunderstorm. Lightning strikes repeatedly around our old farmhouse. One bolt hits the wiring and blows out all the light bulbs in the back half of the house. Another bolt strikes the telephone entrance box; it explodes, scattering melted pieces of plastic and metal throughout the front yard.

We are relieved when the storm passes. After assessing the damage, I go into the kitchen to draw some water. None comes out of the faucet; I discover no water is flowing anywhere in the house.

At first I am not greatly concerned. Our water comes from an old spring located near the top of a hill across the road five hundred feet behind the house. Often a heavy runoff stirs up the reservoir and silt then clogs the intake filter. I climb the hill, check the filter, and discover that it is not at all clogged. "What could be the problem?" I wonder aloud to Sherry, my wife.

She offers her theory, "I think the lightning hit the waterpipe and broke it somewhere between the house and the spring."

"That hardly seems likely," I respond. "The pipe is plastic and buried in the ground; I doubt that it would draw the lightning."

For the rest of the afternoon I proceed according to my own theory. Assuming that the lack of water and the storm are connected only coincidentally I begin to check the line for a break. I know where the pipe is buried, beginning at the spring and running down the steep hill on the far side of the road, because it lies only six inches below the surface there. When she left the house vacant during the winter before Sherry and I bought the farm, the previous owner neglected to drain the water pipes. The inside piping and the pipe that runs from the spring to the house froze and ruptured at several points. The next summer during the first month we lived in the house I had to walk that pipeline looking for water seeping out of the ground, dig it up at each break, and repair it. Recalling that initial experience, I start inspecting the ground where the pipeline is buried looking for a break. I don't find any. The onset of darkness and mosquitoes convinces me to call off the search until the next day. I take some large pails to the river to haul water for the animals.

The new day brings nothing but more frustration. At each point where I dig up the pipeline I can tell that the water is flowing. By the end of the day I reach the bottom of the hill where the pipe goes under the road that lies between the house and the hill. From this point to the house, about two hundred feet away, the pipe is buried six or more feet down. I ask three neighbors who were present when it was originally laid where they think it is located; each describes a different route. No one knows for sure where it is placed. Realizing that it will soon be dark, I suspend the search for another day—and again draw some water from the river for the animals.

The next morning as we stand by the road wondering what to do a friend happens by. When we tell him about our dilemma—how to locate a water pipe buried six feet under the ground eight years earlier—he responds, "Why don't you dowse it?" Sherry is enthusiastic about the idea. He has to leave and can describe only briefly how to dowse with bent wires. I barely manage to conceal my skepticism until he is gone. But I am also tired of carrying water from the river. So I stay and watch as she bends two wires into L shapes and lightly grasps one side of the L near the bent corner in each fist so that the two free sides are parallel to each other and point straight ahead. She walks slowly back and forth along the edge of the road. Each time she crosses a particular spot the wires swing apart and each makes a 180-degree arc until they are again parallel but pointing directly at her. I try holding the wires and walking across the same spot; the wires remain motionless in my hands. She tries again and they swing. She senses my skepticism and offers to hold the wires and close her eyes while I guide her along the road. The wires swing at precisely the same spot as before. I am still skeptical but I have no alternative approach to the problem of locating the water pipe, so I start digging. I dig for almost two hours in the sandy, porous ground. There is no sign of water. Then six feet down my shovel breaks the earth away to reveal a torrent of water coming out of the end of a length of galvanized iron pipe that carries the water under the road. When we shut the water off we discover the remains of a melted plastic coupling in the end of the galvanized pipe. Obviously the lightning had struck the line.

During the years since that lightning strike Sherry has located water pipes many times by dowsing. She has taught others to dowse. Repeatedly she has tried to help me learn how. I cannot do it. As often as I have seen her dowse I cannot do it myself. While I no longer doubt its reality, dowsing remains beyond my capability.

How Deeply Our Perceiving Shapes Our Believing

Several months after we struggled to find the broken water pipe, an article about dowsing appeared in our local newspaper. It was written by a university professor. His research indicates there is no scientific basis for dowsing. He thinks the claims made by dowsers are entirely fabricated and simply play on many people's superstitious nature.

When it comes to dowsing the professor is an unbeliever. Within his cultural world such unbelief is likely to find considerable support. He and his colleagues would no doubt require scientific evidence before they could accept the reality of dowsing. Lacking such evidence, they label dowsing as "unreal" and categorize it as superstition.

Biased believing is an inescapable fact of human experience with which all of us must contend. In *Frameworks*,[1] the first book in this trilogy, I described in detail how human perception is shaped. In the first chapter of this present book, I described how I think our believing is shaped and profoundly biased by our perceiving. In this second chapter I want to describe exactly how that biased shaping takes place and suggest how we can discover counterpoints within the inspiration received by others to counteract the inevitable biases that appear in our own believing.

The incidents I recounted in the opening pages of this chapter illustrate how naturally resistant most of us are to perceptions and beliefs of others that contradict our own. In the face of this natural resistance, it is essential that we admit to the biased nature of our own believing. Our own believing by itself is insufficient. We need to seek inspiration beyond as well as within our own experience. Our faith is likely to be seriously, perhaps dangerously, biased when we trust only own believing and the believing of those who agree with us. We will discover and preserve sound faith only when we seek inspiration beyond as well as within our own believing.

Each of us develops the unique personal characteristics and sensitivities that have been given to us by interacting with our immediate environment. We learn what is noteworthy in the world around us primarily from those with whom we live closely. On the whole we trust them and believe them. While we may resist accepting some of the cues these others (usually family members) provide, what we label as real or unreal depends to a great extent on where, when, and with whom we learn to perceive. As the process of labeling is repeated over and over again, within our experience we learn to designate various phenomena as real or unreal.

What we believe in is conditioned by what these others teach us to perceive and then to label as real. Socialization is the overall term usually employed to describe this labeling process.[2] I often illustrate it with a diagram (fig. 2:1).

Figure 2:1 An Individual Framework

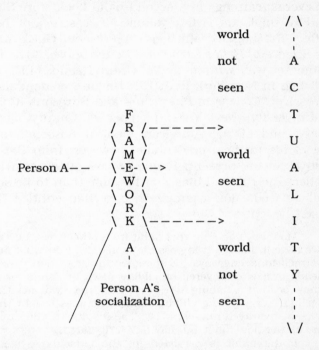

An individual's (Person A in the diagram) personal perspectives taken together compose her or his "framework." That framework takes shape as he or she decides what to see (what is real) and what to overlook (what is not real). Once the framework is well established the individual perceives only what his or her framework admits and no longer sees what he or she has been encouraged and learned and decided to overlook.

The cultures and subcultures within which we are socialized suggest both what we should notice and what we should accept as real or unreal. Usually we are most aware of this discriminating process when we notice the biases of a culture other than our own. But sometimes we become conscious of the extent to which our view of reality has been influenced by our own culture when we encounter beliefs that were once commonly accepted in our own culture but that are now generally discredited.

Several years ago in a second-hand book store Sherry found a single surviving volume of a series of books entitled *The Eugenic Marriage: A Personal Guide to the New Science of Better Living and Better Babies*. The four-volume set was written by W. Grant Hague, M.D. and published in New York in 1916. Hague's credentials are impressive: "College of Physicians and Surgeons (Columbia University) New York; Member of County Medical Society, and of the American Medical Association." In spite of his medical credentials, however, from the perspectives of the present, Hague's views often seem more to reflect the cultural biases of his time than to be scientifically based. For example in a section entitled "Self-Abuse," he writes:

> Most boys acquire this habit from other boys, but as we have intimated it is possible to acquire it in what are termed innocent ways. Sometimes the sensation which leads to it is discovered by sliding down banisters; or it may be that climbing trees or poles first awakens the feeling. Very young children are sometimes taught the vice by depraved nurses. . . . The results are the same no matter how the habit may have originated.
>
> If the habit is persisted in, the muscular system suffers,—the muscles become weak and flabby; the patient develops weariness and loses his mental and physical vigor. He is no longer forceful or energetic, his efficiency is impaired and as a consequence his nervous system begins to show signs of depleted strength. He cannot concentrate his thoughts, he falls behind in his studies, his mental effort is sluggish, he becomes diffident and shy, shuns society, loses confidence in himself, is morbid and emotional and may even think of suicide.
>
> It is astonishing how indulgence in this habit may affect the moral nature of a boy. First of all he is no longer frank and open. He becomes shifty and suspi-

cious and will not look you squarely in the face. A boy cannot become a slave to this habit without it affecting his mind. He invites debasing thoughts,—the old pure and clean method of thought and living no longer satisfy. His imagination even becomes corrupt and his moral nature and moral sense is perverted until he no longer seems able to tell the difference between right and wrong. He has little regard for the truth and if the occasion demands it he will lie without appreciating the dishonorable part he is playing. In the end his will power is lost—even the effort to save himself is too feeble to succeed—he is a slave to the habit, his health and strength ruined.[3]

From the vantage point of the present, it seems astounding that a prestigious physician could have viewed normal sexual developments as Dr. Hague did. Yet such assumptions about the hazards of "self-abuse" were still quite common when I was a boy. Obviously the "scientific" perspectives of this physician were deeply biased by his culture. At least so it seems to most of us today.

The shared perceptual norms of subcultures encourage those who live within them to accept certain perspectives as real and to deny the reality of others. Thus the professor in the newspaper and his colleagues, like the 1916 physician and his contemporaries, affirm cultural frameworks that define for them what constitutes reality—and is, therefore, believable. Though the professor would likely categorize the doctor's explanations as superstitions, each employs culturally defined perspectives (beliefs) to categorize and explain the phenomena he encounters. And each has faith in his cultural framework. A slightly altered diagram portrays such a cultural framework (see fig. 2:2).

Improvements in communication and the proliferation of subcultures within contemporary society have both made us more aware of cultural frameworks. The challenging encounters we have with many around us day by day make the sociocultural basis of our perceiving more apparent than in times past. Rapid and radical social change during this century has provided dramatically different experiences to shape and fix the core perspec-

Figure 2:2 A Cultural Framework

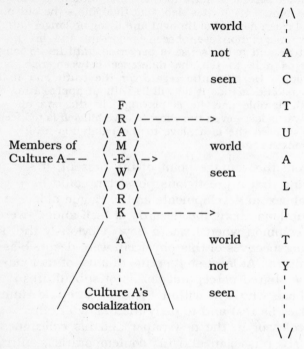

tives of three generations during their formative years. In *Frameworks* I described these unique sets of perspectives that tend to be held by those socialized during three "prime" time periods during the century. The three generations, or cohorts—whom I call Strivers (those socialized during the Great Depression), Challengers (those socialized during the 1960s), and Calculators (those socialized in the late 1970s and 1980s)—now live side-by-side in the present and continue to perceive the world through sets of perceptual norms (frameworks) forged during their own prime times. Begin a discussion on any important subject (war, family, the future, the church, money, God) and you are likely to find sharply different perspectives among the Strivers, Challengers, and Calculators.[4]

Once frameworks are established, they tend to persist. New experiences are interpreted according to the prevailing framework. Even experiences that appear to contradict the framework are often explained away. They may be categorized as exceptions, or the individual believes that access to more complete or accurate information would explain the experience within the accepted framework. Well-established frameworks are very resilient. Even a series of profoundly contradictory experiences is rarely sufficient to undermine our faith in the reality of our framework.

Listening to the Inspiration Within

For those of us who receive faith as a gift from God, that faith is given a particular shape during the process of socialization. In figure 2:3 I have included the dimension of inspiration in my diagram of an individual framework.

Figure 2:3 An Inspired Individual Framework

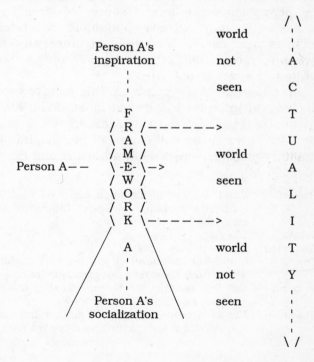

As the diagram implies, I believe our socialization interacts with the inspiration we receive as we form our individual frameworks. All the relationships or associations involved in our socialization give a particular shape to our faith. For example, on the one hand, if we choose not to identify, affiliate with, or participate in any church, our faith is shaped by the perceptions we have as one who stands aside from organized religion. On the other hand, if we identify ourselves with a particular church, and especially when we participate actively in a church, our faith is shaped by the culture of that church.

Our understanding of God originates in the inspiration we receive; but it is given a particular shape by our socialization. Some characteristics of God are clear to us and some are not. We perceive some attributes of God more accurately than others do and some less accurately. Overall we tend to perceive God within images that our culture-based frameworks encourage. That selective perception is at once a source of strength and weakness. We may perceive God more accurately in some ways and not so accurately in other ways. We receive inspiration that others do not; others receive inspiration that we do not.

George Bernard Shaw points up this relative capacity to receive and interpret inspiration in *St. Joan*, his play based on the historical Joan of Arc. In Act 1 Joan is quizzed about the mode and source of her inspiration by two military officers, Robert de Baudricourt and Bertrand de Poulengey.

Robert:	What did you mean when you said that St. Catherine and St. Margaret talked to you every day?
Joan:	They do.
Robert:	What are they like?
Joan:	[*suddenly obstinate*] I will tell you nothing about that: they have not given me leave.
Robert:	But you actually see them; and they talk to you just as I am talking to you?
Joan:	No: it is quite different. I cannot tell you: you must not talk to me about my voices.

Robert:	How do you mean? voices?
Joan:	I hear voices telling me what to do. They come from God.
Robert:	They come from your imagination.
Joan:	Of course. That is how the messages of God
Poulengey:	Checkmate.[5]

The inspiration Joan receives is not apparent to the two soldiers; in fact, it does not seem at all real to them. It lies beyond the boundaries of their frameworks. As a result they are faced with a dilemma: either they must deny the reality of her inspiration (as the professor denied the reality of dowsing), or they must admit that it is real but beyond the realm of their experience (as I did when I was unable to dowse). Of course, given their inability to believe in her inspiration, Joan also faces a choice: will she continue to believe in and follow the leading of "voices" that only she hears?

The play provides a dramatic illustration of choices we all face. Faith at times provides us with inspired insights that others do not perceive, and may suggest courses of action they do not affirm. The inspiration that comes to us in such moments is often challenging: should we heed the inspiration, the "voices," that few others, and sometimes no one else, hears?

Just over a decade ago, when I was in my middle forties, I resigned my position as a denominational executive. I knew I was called to move on, though I wasn't certain to what. For a time I traveled, making my living as a full-time church-strategy consultant. That initial shift in ministry went surprisingly well; I seemed to be helpful to congregations and denominational units with which I worked. I had more requests for consultations than I could respond to.

That new direction seemed logical to most of my friends. Fifteen years previously I had been called away from the pastorate of a small, country church to assume the post of senior minister in a large, urban congregation Two and one-half years later I had been called from that position to assume the ministry of a synod executive.

During that ministry I completed a graduate degree in sociology. As a strategy consultant I drew on all my previous experience; to most people who knew me then, it seemed like a very appropriate ministry for me. They expected that I would continue as a full-time consultant for the foreseeable future.

The new direction my life now took did not seem to my friends to be clearly a matter of calling. In fact, when Sherry and I decided to move away from the inner city to a small farm in rural Maine, some of my colleagues wondered about my motives. Few seemed sympathetic when I explained that I felt called to reduce my consulting in order to have time to understand and, it is to be hoped, address the difficulties we Christians face as we seek to discover and share faith today. Most listened politely, though it was clear many did not appreciate or agree with the direction my life was now taking. Some thought I was "burned out." A few saw the move as an evasion of responsibility. One person said he felt I was turning my back on my gifts. Though these questioners gave me some moments of uncertainty, the voices within me urged me ahead. Now that I am well settled into teaching and writing and have watched the pieces of my life fall into place, it is easier to recognize that God was beckoning in those initial stirrings.

There are occasions in our lives when we are challenged to heed the "voices" only we hear. In such moments each of us needs to say to herself or himself, "Others tell me what they see I should be; I experience what I am called to be." At such times the direction of our lives can be explained only by the inspiration within our own experience, and sometimes that inspiration is apparent only to us. History abounds with examples of believers who attended to inspiration that no one or only a few of their contemporaries appreciated—from Ruth and Mary Magdalene, Hosea and Jesus, to St. Francis and St. Teresa, Roger Schutz of Taizé and Mother Teresa of Calcutta, and countless others whose names we neither know nor can recall.

Though most of us are numbered among the "count-less others" who are unknown, meeting the challenge of the inspiration given to us is no less momentous in God's sight. We are likely to find fullness of faith only as we honor our own experience of God. Our faith needs to be anchored in the unique inspiration God gives to us.

Listening to the Inspiration of Others

Our faith also needs to be balanced by challenges that originate beyond our own personal experience. We are most likely to find fullness of faith as we bring our own knowledge of God into dialogue with perceptions of God that lie beyond our usual experience. Fullness of faith comes to us as we search not only within but also beyond our usual believing, beyond our unbelief, beyond our frameworks. Our inspired perception, like all our perception, is always partial. We all see, as Paul observed, only a portion of reality (1 Cor. 13:12). Fullness of faith comes to those who are willing to hear the voices beyond their own experience as well as the voices within.

The pluralism of American society, with its many subcultures composed of persons with widely varied frameworks, has made the partial and often biased nature of our perspectives more apparent. Many of us now recognize that the vision given to any one of us is partial as well as unique. We accept the fact that even our inspired images of God are *always* limited, *always* less than perfect.

What we know of God is, as Shaw's *St. Joan* suggests, only what we can imagine from our experience. Personal experience can be deceptive as well as insightful. We all can recall incidents in which we interpreted an experience as it happened and then discovered we had to revise our understanding on the basis of new insight. Similarly, in a long relationship we sometimes discover that a person is quite different from what we initially imagined him or her to be. Our current image of God may also include elements based on early misapprehensions. Like all other reality in our experience, sometimes we distort the inspiration that comes to us from God. Seminary students commonly complain about "losing their faith" when they gain intellectual tools that enable them to reflect critically on beliefs they have carried from childhood. Beliefs about God that are based on childish misapprehensions do not stand up under critical reflection. And they should not.

On July 19, 1989, the engine mounted in the tail of a DC-10 airliner exploded in flight. Pieces of metal severed the aircraft's hydraulic systems. As a result the pilot lost nearly all of his ability to control the airplane. He was able to maneuver it only by varying the speed of the remaining two engines. With great skill he guided the airplane to the Sioux City, Iowa, airport for a landing. His lack of control forced him to land the airplane at a high rate of speed; a wing caught the ground, flipping the plane over. It broke apart and burned. More than one hundred of those on board were killed. Among those who escaped from the wreckage was a flight attendant who crawled through an opening in the burning wreckage. A news report quoted her father's description of her experience.

> She said she was tumbling. The walls were coming in.
> She said a hole opened up and the sunlight came in and
> she climbed out the hole. She said she knew the Lord
> opened up that hole.[6]

In interviews held after the disaster many surviving passengers described prayers in which they asked God to spare them or expressed thanksgiving that God had spared them.[7] While I can certainly understand the immense relief someone feels who survives such a disaster, I also think it is important to challenge the belief that God intervened to open a hole in a burning airplane to enable one person to climb to safety—while permitting more than a hundred others to perish in the flames. As common as such responses are on the part of those who survive close calls with disaster, I cannot help but wonder whether the image of God implied in their perspective on the experience is accurate. It seems reasonable to assume that many of those who died also prayed that they would be spared. Why the special treatment for some and not others?

Bias slips easily into pictures of God based only on our own or our own group's perspectives. These biased perspectives may encourage the believer to interpret God through the events of his or her life in terms that are self-serving. While such self-serving understandings of God and what God wants can be relatively harmless, they may also encourage questionable, even abusive, behavior.

Several years ago two of my son's friends, a young woman and young man who were soon to be married, were encouraged by their pastor to attend a weekend retreat designed to prepare prospective wives and husbands for the roles they were to assume as Christian marriage partners. When they returned, the young woman reported that she now understood why she would promise to "obey" her husband in the marriage ceremony and why she should look upon him as her "lord." She has, in fact, continued to function in their marriage in the submissive role suggested by her and her congregation's literal interpretation of some scriptural references to marriage (e.g. Eph. 5:22-24).

Insisting that women cast themselves in such a submissive role is demeaning. It is also risky. The dangers to which she exposes herself when a wife adopts such a submissive attitude may become sadly apparent when her husband turns out to be less than Christlike in his beliefs and actions. While, thankfully, my son's friend does not abuse his wife, countless cases of spouse abuse and child abuse, even by those who identify themselves as Christian, testify to the hazard of refusing to recognize that inspired faith is shaped by personal and cultural biases—even the inspiration that stands behind scripture. Not long ago on a Sunday morning as he drove by a local church, a friend came upon a man beating a young child in the yard outside the church. He was so stunned by the vehemence of the beating that he stopped his car and walked over to interfere. A woman who said she was the child's mother stood in his way. When he questioned her about the beating, she explained that the child had misbehaved in the worship service. The beating was "good for" the child, the woman explained. He was being taught to fear God and to honor his father and mother. Some day, she said, the child would thank the man for beating respect for God into him.

Paul's attitudes toward women and children (and slavery) reflect the culture in which he lived. To insist that our attitudes and behavior toward women and children today should be guided only by Paul's understanding of God denies that Paul's inspiration was culturally conditioned and renders them unnecessarily vulnerable to abuse. Such a narrow perspective also discounts the reality of continuing inspiration. Some of us who are inspired today will perceive God's character and intentions more clearly in some respects than those who lived two thousand years ago.

The realization that each of us is responsible for the theological accuracy of his or her believing will probably make some of us uneasy, at least initially. When seminary students gain tools that enable them to reflect critically on their believing and then complain they are "losing their faith," actually they are being challenged to become mature believers. Paul suggests that adult believing requires us to put away childish believing (1 Cor. 13:11–12). He also suggests that mature believing involves a cooperative relationship with God, one in which we take some responsibility for our salvation (Phil. 2:12–13). Paul's own believing involves a great deal of critical reflection on the faith that he received as his letters repeatedly indicate, especially Romans, Galatians, and Ephesians. His letters also reveal that a challenging dialogue went on between Paul, his followers, and the Jerusalem church (and that Paul did not always participate in these conversations gracefully—c.f. Galatians 5:12, where he wishes that his opponents would mutilate themselves).

Being open to the challenges of perspectives beyond our own can bring needed balance to our believing. One point at which the personal believing of many of us needs to be challenged today concerns the language we use to refer to God. Many of us have narrow male images of God—and consequently of the relative capacities of women and men to fulfill our models of godliness. We need to broaden our images by employing sexually neutral terms. If we use masculine terms, we need to complement them with feminine terms to bring balance to our language and imagery. As important as these changes are, I think we need to go even further. It seems to me that all the anthropomorphic terms we customarily use to describe God are less potent in today's English than they were in the languages and cultures of those who wrote the scripture. God when described in these terms today appears considerably less awesome, and by implication more manageable, than the "lord" of the Old and New Testaments.

Words such as father and lord and king conveyed a sense of unrestricted power in scriptural times (which is one reason it is dangerous to imply uncritically that such terms are suitable models for male humans today). The patriarchal fathers and kings of the Old Testament and the lords of the societies within which the New Testament writers lived were omnipotent sovereigns who held life–and–death power over their subjects. As such they could serve as models from which to infer the scope and depth of God's power. To use "father" or "lord" or "king" to refer to God today implies much less than it did then. Most kings today are ceremonial figures who have little actual power; the inhabitants of their realms hardly feel (or act) like subjects. Fathers are often portrayed in the popular media as rather inept comical characters. For many of us the words lord or lordship or father call forth the image of someone who is quaint or comical. These quaint and domestic connotations that may be associated with traditional terms for God can mislead us into believing that God wants to have a cozy relationship with us. Our faith becomes overly informal; our God is too small. Forgetting (or unaware of) the profound and expansive connotations the words father and lord held in the culture of those who chose them to describe God in the scripture, we may imagine God as someone akin to a cosmic daddy or mommy who gives us special attention—with little appreciation of the implications of such a limited picture of God. Within such a perspective, God may become a cosmic parent who singles us out for special consideration, providing for our escape from tight spots while others perish.

The overwhelming evidence within and beyond scripture indicates that no one is especially privileged in God's sight, that God's care is unconditionally available to all. I once heard a Roman Catholic priest describe his own encounter with a near disaster on an airplane. One of the landing gears would not lock into position. As the plane circled the airport, the pilot issued instructions to prepare the passengers for a crash landing. Fire engines lined the runway. The airplane landed ever so lightly. The landing gear held; no one was hurt. As he disembarked from the airplane, the priest's eyes met those of a flight attendant. He felt called upon to say something theologically "profound" to her to fit the occasion. He said, "The rest of your life is a gift."

She replied, "Father, I thought life was a gift to begin with."

Sometimes those we least expect to do so confront us with a new perspective that brings a helpful balance to our believing. Mature believing necessarily requires an ongoing critical dialogue between our own faith experience and the faith experiences of others—including those experiences recorded in the scripture and historical tradition we have received. To participate in that dialogue we must be prepared to challenge and to be challenged.

The motion picture *Mass Appeal* recounts the struggle of an older priest and a younger deacon to appreciate each other's perspectives. They come from two different

cultures in time. The older priest is a Striver, unques-
tioningly committed to maintaining the institutional
church. The deacon is a Challenger, mercilessly pointing
up the church's inability to respond to issues of social
change and social justice. As the story unfolds, each
discovers some of the shortsightedness in his own framework and some of the wisdom in the other's. In a dramatic moment when the rector of the deacon's seminary
has decided to expel him, the old priest affirms the
deacon's challenging perspectives with the question: "Don't
we have an obligation to shape the church that has
shaped us?" Yes we do. And often the suggestions
needed to reshape the beliefs we have accepted come
from without.

Nurturing the Balancing Rhythm

What steps can we take to establish and maintain a
dialogue between our own and others' perceptions of God
that will bring a balancing rhythm to our believing?

I believe an essential first step is to open ourselves to
those who might be able to help us grow in faith, especially when we find ourselves in circumstances where
our believing is likely to benefit from those whose inspiration and perspectives differ from our own.

Some years ago at the opening dinner of a national-
church board meeting, I was seated next to a man who
had just passed through a personal tragedy. Only a
month before, his wife and two children had been killed
in a car accident. I could see he was still in shock. But
he insisted that his faith in God had not been shaken at
all by the tragedy. Quite the opposite; though at first he
had been tempted to question, the words of his minister
at the funeral had put a stop to his doubts.

"What did your minister say that was so helpful?" I
asked.

A controlled smile came across his face as he replied:
"He said I should rejoice!"

"Why?" I wondered in open amazement.

"Because, as my minister explained to me, 'No human touched them. The car slid on the ice and hit a tree. Since no human intervened, it was obviously a direct action of God. Therefore, you have no need to doubt or grieve; you can simply rejoice that they are now with God.' Isn't that wonderful?"

"I don't think so—not at all," was my immediate gut response.

"Why not?"

I went on: "If God acted the way your minister suggests, then I am afraid I would hate God."

A tear in his eye began the grieving he had stifled. We talked for a long time.

When we are under great stress we may not have the capacity to resist the suggestions of those whose theological perspective is distorted. We may even embrace beliefs that in better moments we would realize are inadequate or harmful to our faith. At such times it is important to share what we believe with another Christian we respect and trust, especially if we find ourselves uneasy or defensive about our perspectives. We may discover in the other's response the counterpoint needed to supplement or correct our own believing. I am often struck by the large proportion of Christians who seem to think that the only role or most appropriate role they should adopt in their relationship with God is to be compliant and passive. These believers seem to me to function like dependent children who have never grown up in faith to take responsibility for their own believing. I think these passive believers are especially vulnerable to strong personalities who may misguide them.

Scripture abounds with strong personalities who obviously think they have both the right and the obligation to take some responsibility for their own believing. Many (e.g. Sarah, Moses, Jeremiah, Peter, the woman at the well) are quite assertive in their encounters with God or Jesus. They take the risk of reaching beyond their own inspiration, and they often discover richer faith as they come in contact with God through inspiration that lies outside their current framework.

The conversation Nicodemus seeks with Jesus is a case in point (John 3). Nicodemus has a limited perception of the Spirit of God. His framework reflects the perspectives of the culture within which he lives. He seeks the conversation with Jesus because he senses his (and his culture's) inadequacy. In that conversation, Jesus pushes Nicodemus beyond his framework. When he struggles against its limits, Jesus likens the Spirit to the wind in order to help Nicodemus reach beyond the limits of his usual perceiving. "The wind blows where it chooses, and you hear the sound of it, but you do not know where it comes from or where it goes. So it is with everyone who is born of the Spirit." When Nicodemus still balks, Jesus says, in effect, "Believe in my faith," or in Jesus' words, "we speak of what we know, and testify to what we have seen [John 3:11]."

The richness of living among Christians with different cultural frameworks emerges when we view those who hold perspectives that differ from ours not as adversaries but as potential collaborators. Our faith can grow not only when we defend it but when we modify it.

Both Nicodemus and the man who lost his family in that tragic accident faced dilemmas that were beyond their own inspired believing. They reached within themselves and their cultural frameworks for inspiration and found none. The needed inspiration came through others when they reached beyond themselves. They both found reaching out difficult, even frightening, but they found through another the inspiration needed to enrich their believing.

To rest our faith entirely on inspiration that falls within or on inspiration that is ordinarily beyond our usual perception constrains our believing. We are much more likely to find a full, balanced faith as we move back and forth in an enabling rhythm between the inspiration we receive within our own framework and the challenging, enriching inspiration we receive from sources that lie beyond it. God comes to us both from within and without.

CHAPTER 3

Embracing God's Endless, Bounded Love

March 6 is a holy day for Sherry and me; it is the day we were married. Every March 6 brings recollections of our first March 6. As each hour of the day passes, I relive in my memory the events that occurred during that same hour years ago.

I recall waking early to a bright sun. When I go outside the air feels unusually warm for a late winter's day. I stop at a familiar flower shop near the city brownstone Sherry has just finished restoring, and buy a handful of daisies. I see Sherry for the first time in the hundred-year-old wedding dress she has decided to wear for the occasion. She and I pin the same lace on it that graced the wedding dress of the grandmother who raised her. I take a picture of Sherry lacing her boots. We walk in the sun to the downtown church where we worship. Save for a minister-friend, we stand alone at the front of a huge sanctuary and commit ourselves to each other.

Though these memories of our covenanting are particularly vivid each March 6, I am often conscious at other times of the intimacy that has grown between us. This intimacy is nurtured both by the devotion that constitutes the center of our relationship and the commitment that forms its boundaries. The intimacy I share with Sherry I share with no one else. Ours is not an "open marriage." Nor do I want it to be. We honor the old vow; we "cleave to each other only." We know it is safe to abandon ourselves unreservedly to this marriage in the center of our lives because we are committed to its

45

boundaries. We are so sustained by our relationship because we are willing to be constrained by it.

On our anniversary each year we recall and remake our covenant: we say again to each other the vows we first made on our wedding day. Each year the old vows hold even more meaning for us. We have known the strength that comes with health, and we have supported each other through frightening illnesses. We have survived times when we did not have enough money, and we have enjoyed times of abundance. We have shared great joys and deep sorrows. We now renew our vows in anticipation deepened by experience.

Seeing Through the Bible to God

My relationship with Sherry is a human reflection of the relationship I experience with God. I believe God seeks to establish such a relationship with all of us. God is like a lover who wants us to love in return. In fact, God has already taken the initiative to establish a loving relationship with us.

Many of us find it surprisingly difficult to appreciate how deeply God is committed to us. We find it hard to imagine that God is actually like a lover who wants to give more to us than we can give in return, or that God persists in loving us even when we are not faithful.

Scripture is a record of God's initiatives and of the relationships that develop between God and those who respond to those initiatives. Scripture traces women's and men's struggles on the one hand to accept the boundless nature of God's love and on the other to honor the boundaries of faithfulness.

Scripture is full of good news about God's boundless love. Unfortunately, many of us are not as certain about the reliability of what we read in scripture as we would like to be. From our present-day perspective some of the key stories in the Bible that describe God's character and activity, like the stories of Creation and the flood that covered the earth, seem more like fantasy than reality.

Various aspects of the character of God as revealed in scripture seem at odds with one another. We come away from the Bible unsure whether scripture gives us a dependable and coherent picture of God. Is God as portrayed in scripture a reality or a fantasy—or some mixture of the two?

I suspect that many of us find it difficult to believe that scripture offers reliable revelation for two reasons:

First, the way we were taught to approach the scripture causes difficulties for some of us. As I suggested in chapters 1 and 2, some of us were encouraged to place the women and men of scripture on a level above ordinary human beings. We were encouraged to attribute a level of perfection to the inspiration received by those who wrote the Bible that we would never assume for ourselves or even for the most inspired believers who live today. We were led to believe that Christians think scripture is uniquely qualified to set the standard for believing because scripture is without error. But, as I have suggested, the fact that scripture is inspired does not mean that those who wrote scripture were free from error.

If we want to appreciate fully the important insights the biblical narrators can offer us, we will have to resist any temptation to idolize them. As I suggested, I believe the women and men we meet in the Bible received inspiration within the limits of their frameworks just as we do. While I do *not* mean to imply that God is flawed, I *do* think that *all* human believers, even the most inspired, perceive God, at times, inaccurately. Sometimes the biblical narrators understood the revelation they received accurately, and sometimes they misunderstood. They were profoundly inspired humans, but because they were humans, we need to scrutinize their perceptions of God, just as we do our own. Scripture is historical as well as inspired. It records not only the narrators' accurate perceptions and understanding of the nature of God but also their inaccurate perceptions of God and their struggles against these mistaken percep-

tions.   To receive the full benefit of their profound insights, we need to accept the fact that they sometimes
misunderstood—and to recognize those misunderstandings for what they are: misunderstandings based on misperceptions.   I believe we are most likely to gain an
accurate understanding of God when we consider their
inspiration critically in the light of our own.

Second, the means the biblical narrators employ to
present their evidence diminishes its credibility for some
of us. Those who share their experiences in the pages of
scripture often describe the essential character of God in
symbolic stories. When we read these stories from our
cultural perspective, they do *not* help establish the reality
of God on firm ground for many of us. The effect is often
quite the opposite: they make God seem more like a
character in a fairy tale than someone real.

To appreciate how biblical stories can convey reliable
and accurate insight into the nature of God, we will need
to learn how to accept and look past the limitations of
the culture in which the stories are set. And some of us
also will need to set aside our belief that important
truths can be reliably demonstrated only (or best) through
philosophical argument, scientific proof, or historical fact.
These common methods of our culture were largely unfa-
miliar to those we meet in the scripture.

The Old Testament narrators told stories to describe
what God is like and how God relates to creation because the most common descriptive models they could
draw on to portray God and the creation were spiritual
and relational. They naturally envisioned the workings
of creation in relational, not mechanical, terms. Creation
begins when God decides to create, and creation continues to function as it does because God sustains it. The
key dynamics of creation are the purposes God is carrying out. Their central concern is to show how God is
involved in the creation, how God wishes to care for us,
and how God wants us to care for one another and the
creation.

The Old Testament storytellers have little interest in
understanding or explaining the mechanics of creation.

They seem unaware of or unconcerned about inconsistencies that raise difficult questions for those of us who are trained to focus on scientific or historical detail. They can comfortably set stories side by side that contain serious contradictions from our perspective, and feel no discomfort at all. When we think that we must evaluate the reliability of their stories in terms of our scientific or historical criteria, we are likely either to reject the stories as a whole or to involve ourselves in attempts to redefine the details so they appear to be consistent. We focus and stumble on inconsistencies that were of little concern to them and miss the essential truths they intend to convey, truths that many of us long to believe.

Consider, for example, the two Creation stories that open the book of Genesis. The first story, which appears in Genesis 1, describes an orderly creation of the universe over six days with the seventh day set aside for rest. God makes the heavens and the earth; the sun, moon, and stars; plants and animals; and, finally, humans. At first glance, it appears that this account of creation might agree with contemporary scientific theories concerning the origin and order of the universe. But this apparent agreement quickly dissolves with closer reading. The narrative implies, for example, that God placed the stars in the heavens and the sun and moon into their orbits on the fourth day, the day *after* the plants and trees were made. How could plants have emerged, let alone survived, without the sun? We are now face to face with the kind of dilemma we encounter when we evaluate the scripture from our own cultural perspective.

An older Creation narrative, which is recorded in Genesis 2 and 3, compounds our difficulty. While this story complements the first and offers vital insights into the nature of God and the nature of our relationship with God and the creation, the order of creation it portrays is even more scientifically preposterous than that described in the first story. God begins by making a man (literally, "an earthling") out of the dust of the earth. God then makes vegetation as a gift to sustain man and for him to enjoy. Next God makes the animals and the birds. Finally God makes a woman. The humans are given a lush garden and each other to enjoy. They are creatures *within* the created order, not, as the serpent suggests, above it as God is. To continue to enjoy the benefits of creation, they must respect the limits within which they are created, limits symbolized in the tree of the knowledge of good and evil. When they fail to do so, they bring disaster upon themselves and all they touch. The world that was created good is filled with evil.

From our present-day perspective, some of the details in these stories seem scientifically impossible, and some of the social attitudes they assume are not acceptable. The older story that appears in Genesis 2 and 3 is especially difficult. The order in which creation occurs—man first, vegetation second, animals and birds third, woman last—contradicts most modern theories about the origin of the creation, as well as the order described in the first Creation story. This older story is also blatantly sexist, reflecting the sexist perspectives that dominated ancient Israel. Evil is introduced into the world through the weakness of the woman. She is naively beguiled by the serpent and becomes the cause of man's failing. This lapse reveals her inherit inferiority and justifies making her subordinate to man.

To try to resolve the tension between the details of these stories and our cultural and scientific perspectives is both futile and unnecessary. The biblical storytellers lacked twentieth-century scientific data that are available to us, and they shaped their stories within the biases of their culture. Neither the scientific nor the cultural perspectives of the biblical writers are inspired. They never intended to communicate "scientific" data, in the sense that we commonly use this word. As a result, when we read their stories from our twentieth-century vantage point, their scientific assumptions are understandably inaccurate. Some of their cultural attitudes seem obnoxious to many of us as well. Those who insist that all the scientific details and cultural attitudes that appear in scripture are inspired by God make it difficult for many of us to accept the profound theological insights that scripture does have to offer.

To appreciate what the biblical narrators can tell us about God, we need to focus on the theological insight they give us and overlook the inaccurate details and cultural perspectives that bias their stories. When we do so, we discover that the theological insights are still vital. They describe accurately what God is like, how God is involved in the creation, how we humans fit in to God's order, how God will relate to us, and how we can relate to God.

The first story reveals that God is the ultimate source of all life. God is the creator of all that is. God is good. All that God creates is good. There is an established order to creation. Humans are created and placed within God's order. Like all else in God's creation, we are essentially good.

The story that appears second clarifies the implications of our dominant status as humans in the created order. It shows how the presence of evil within and around us compounds our responsibilities. Though its origins remain cloaked in mystery, evil (represented by the serpent) is a reality. Our nature remains basically good, but it is corrupted. We still have the ability to direct our own lives and to affect one another's lives and the life of the creation as a whole. But we can exercise that power for ill as well as for good. The point of the narrative is clear: we must recognize that we are stewards, not gods, and honor the obligations and boundaries that accompany our status within the order God has established. When we, like Adam and Eve, violate the boundaries God sets for us, we bring disaster upon ourselves and the entire creation. We humans and all other forms of life have to live with the consequences of our actions.

The ancient stories that appear in the opening chapters of Genesis describe the nature and the limits of creation with surprising accuracy. They describe our human condition precisely as well. While we may question the scientific assumptions and cultural biases the stories reflect, what they suggest about the essential nature of God, the created order, and human beings is accurate and believable and important.

God, a Persistent Lover

The tragic blight of evil that spoils the creation and human beings does not frustrate God's intention for them. Quite the opposite. God not only refuses to stop caring; God initiates a plan designed to help humans and the creation recover their wholeness. God even invites humans to join in extending this healing to the creation. The story of the Great Flood focuses on the unalterable character of God's love. The calling of Abraham reveals God's plan to share the vitality of godliness with everyone.

The story of the Great Flood (Gen. 9:8-17) establishes the persistence of God's caring in a world now filled with evil. Some of us may need to rethink our original responses to the details of the story to appreciate the important insight it provides. Images of animals going two by two into the ark can make the flood story seem like only a fantasy. The discovery that other ancient cultures passed down similar flood stories may also discourage some of us from taking the story seriously. The story is not unique to the Bible.

Perhaps the most difficult obstacle the story presents is the way God is portrayed at the beginning. God simply runs out of patience with humans. With the exception of one virtuous man and his family, and the other living things they save, God destroys all living beings.

Again we need to be aware of the cultural perspectives and biases of the biblical narrators. As they struggled to discern and then describe the nature of God, they often likened God to the most powerful people around them. As I said in the last chapter, sometimes they attributed the same questionable human traits to God that were typical of the most powerful earthly lords they observed. We need to test the images of God presented in these early records against the character of God that emerges in scripture as a whole, and consider them in the light of our own experience of God. If we recognize these early capricious characteristics as misperceptions, I think we are better able to appreciate the central, inspired insight the flood story offers. God promises never again to run out of patience with humans and destroy them and all other life. God's abiding nature is clear. God's caring can never be frustrated or altered by the evil humans do.

The biblical narrators use the word covenant to establish God's commitment as irrevocable. The imagery associated with making a covenant in the Old Testament is potent. The Hebrew verb we translate as "make" in the phrase "make a covenant" is literally the verb "cut" in the original. It was commonly used in connection with stone cutting. The intended image is plain: God's commitment is etched in stone. It cannot be erased. God is committed forever to the promise given in the covenant. God will never destroy the creation. Nothing we or anyone else does can change God's commitment.

God's promise to Abraham reveals an even deeper commitment on God's part. God will *actively* bless the creation. This additional promise to Abraham declares that God will actively communicate healing love to the creation and that God calls humans to become the means to carry this healing. The dynamic of God's caring love is built into the created order. The implications of the promise to Abraham are startling: Humans can be blessed with the soul of God. "'I will bless you, and make your name great, so that you will be a blessing. . . . and in you all the families of the earth shall be blessed' [Gen. 12:2, 3]."

We feel the full impact of this statement only when we appreciate the force it carries in the original Hebrew. The English word blessing fails to convey the powerful reality to which the Hebrew word (*berakha*) points. This Hebrew word, which we translate as "bless," assumes a dynamic similar to the one we associate with the word curse. When someone says, "I will put a curse on Mary," or "Mary is under a curse," the statement suggests that Mary is under the spell of the curse. If the curse is potent, and Mary is under its spell, something tangible will happen to her. How effective the curse will be depends on the powers the curser possesses. The more potent the person who gives the curse, the more powerful its effects are likely to be.

For most of us, the feelings associated with the word curse are a carryover from former times when more people accepted the reality of curses. Few of us who live in present-day American culture actually believe in curses. But we can still feel the dynamic the word curse connotes. If we recall those feelings and imagine a good curse, we can begin to appreciate the reality to which the biblical word blessing points.

The trickery described in the story of the blessing of Jacob (Gen. 27) illustrates the tangible effects the Hebrews believed were conveyed by a blessing. Isaac, son of Abraham, is an old man. Sensing he may soon die, Isaac asks his older son, Esau, to shoot some game, cook it, and bring it to him to eat. After the meal, he will give his blessing to Esau.

Rebekah, Isaac's wife, has a different plan in mind. Isaac's younger son, Jacob, is her favorite, not Esau. She concocts a plan to deceive Isaac into blessing Jacob instead of Esau. She suggests that Jacob take advantage of Isaac's dim vision. If Jacob acts quickly, he can kill some game, prepare a meal for Isaac, and receive Isaac's blessing before his brother returns. Though Isaac is nearly blind, Jacob is still afraid of the trick. If Isaac recognizes the attempt to deceive him, Jacob fears that his father will be angry and curse him rather than bless him. But Rebekah convinces Jacob that she has thought of all the possible ways the plan might fail. Jacob dresses in his brother's clothes, covers his hands and neck with the "skins of kids" so he will appear to be hairy like his brother, and takes the food that Rebekah prepares to his father. The deception is successful. Isaac gives his blessing to Jacob.

When Esau returns and discovers how Jacob has duped his father, the actual reality a blessing carries is painfully apparent in his outcry and his father's response. Something irreversible has happened. He has lost out.

> When Esau heard his father's words, he cried out with an exceedingly great and bitter cry, and said to his father, "Bless me, me also, father!" But he said, "Your brother came deceitfully, and he has taken away your blessing." . . . Then he [Esau] said, "Have you not reserved a blessing for me?" Isaac answered Esau, "I have already made him your lord, and I have given him all his brothers as servants, and with grain and wine I have sustained him. What then can I do for you, my son?"
>
> —Genesis 27:34-37

Once given the blessing cannot be retrieved. The person who has received it has been changed by it.

The reality transmitted in a blessing can have profound effects on the one who receives it. The one blessed receives the powers of the soul of the blessor. The slang phrase "soul power" is probably the closest approximation available in English to describe what is transmitted in a blessing. In his monumental work *Israel: Its Life and Culture*, Johannes Pedersen describes how a blessing communicates the soul power of the blessor to another. Soul power includes both the core of someone's being *and* the effects that person has on others.

> The soul is a whole saturated with power. It is the same power which acts in the centre and far out in the periphery, as far as the soul extends. . . . This vital power, without which no living being can exist, is called by the Israelites, *berakha*, blessing. The Israelite does not distinguish between the power, as it acts in the soul, and as it manifests itself outwardly. For him [or her] the capacity and the result is the same: where the capacity exists, the result of its action is a matter of course. . . .

> Blessing is the inner strength of the soul and the happiness [well-being, wholeness] it creates.
>
> The act of blessing another, *berekh*, means to communicate to him [her] strength of soul. . . . He [she] who blesses another gives him [her] something of his [her] own soul. . . .
>
> The blessing connects the souls, and so it must be, because it consists in a communication of the contents of the soul.[1]

We can now appreciate the extraordinary implications of God's commitment to Abraham, "I will bless you, and make your name great, so that you will be a blessing. . . . and by you all the families of the earth shall bless themselves." In the promise God makes to Abraham, the soul power of God is communicated *and committed* (recall the irreversible blessing of Jacob) to Abraham, and through Abraham to all the families of the earth. Those whom Abraham and his followers bless share in the blessing Abraham has received from God. Through them the vitality of God's healing love becomes available within the created order.

The continuing vitality of the soul power of God is immediately apparent in the words and actions of Jesus. "Now after John was arrested, Jesus came into Galilee, preaching good news about God, and saying, 'This is the time you have been waiting for, the soul power of God is at your fingertips; change your hearts and minds and believe this good news' [Mark 1:14, 15, author's trans.]." After inviting two brothers, Simon and Andrew, to leave their fishing and join him in his ministry, Jesus goes into a synagogue and acts out the good news. He drives the destructive spirit out of a possessed man. Those who watch are "astounded." They wonder, "What is this?" And then answer their own question with a startled, almost sarcastic outburst, "'A new teaching! [Hardly.] He has the soul power to command even unclean spirits, and they obey him' [Mark 1:27, author's trans.]."

The Greek word I have rendered as "soul power" in this sentence from Mark's Gospel is *eksousia*. It means literally "out of being." Jesus is not simply another religious teacher who talks about God; God is actively present in his being (soul). He touches person after person with that healing power, bringing wholeness to their lives, demonstrating the continuing reality of God's caring.

Jesus invites others to join with him in sharing God's care. He challenges those first two fishermen with the words, "Come along with me and I will teach you how to fish out people." They leave their work and go with him. Over the months they live with him, at his hands they discover the reality of God's blessing. As they are blessed by Jesus, their faith grows, and soon the blessing of God reaches others through their ministries.

A central message emerges from the scripture: God's blessing is real. It is still real. We can receive its benefits when others care for us. When we are blessed by those who believe the good news about God, who have opened their lives to God, the grace we receive through their ministry can reflect God's blessing. When we place our faith in God, the care we extend to others can be enriched by the soul power of God that touches us. In the strength of God's blessing our caring is more than what we could expect from ourselves.

The soul power of God shared through our care for one another is not to be reserved only for good people. Jesus lavishes healing grace on person after person without requiring any of them to meet prescribed conditions in order to receive it. There are no moral or religious prerequisites we need meet in order to be blessed by God. Though faithfulness to God includes honoring stringent boundaries (as will be noted later in this chapter), the availability of God's care is not dependent on our behavior.

It is also clear in Jesus' ministry that God's blessing is available to ordinary people. It is not given only to "important," heroic Christians to enable them to carry out great acts of faith. God's blessing is as pervasive as the rain that falls "on the just and the unjust." Even those whom Jesus invites to become disciples are mostly ordinary people. The soul power of God is readily available to enhance the caring of ordinary people of faith. God blesses people like you and me.

We may not recognize how we have been blessed until some event in our lives moves us to marvel at what we have become. Several years ago one of my daughters fell in love with a young man. Their love showed all the freshness and vitality a sixteen-year-old and an eighteen-year-old can bring to love. It was delightful to watch them discover each other—until she announced one evening that they had decided to get an apartment. She was going to leave home and move in with him.

An array of reasons to oppose her plans quickly surfaced in my mind: I struggled with the ethics of their proposal, especially in light of their ages. He had just graduated from high school. He had found a good job, but it was a summer "boom-time" job in an unstable industry. She had another year of high school. She said she intended to finish, but would she? I wondered what would happen if they had a child? Would she then be able to complete high school? And go on to college, as she had always planned? With parental vision, I looked into her future: Would her passion fade in a year or so? Would she then feel trapped, and regret her hasty decision? Would what she wanted to do now undermine the best use of her God-given gifts in the long run? As I continued to think about her plans, my list of arguments against her proposal grew longer.

In spite of their obvious (to me) logic, when I shared my arguments with my daughter, they did not sound compelling even to my ear. Her reactions quickly let me know that they certainly did not sound compelling to her. I was simply raising issues that had already occurred to her. Lack of awareness on her part was not the problem. We had looked at the same issues and come to different conclusions. I recognized that pressing my points would only stiffen her resistance. I might be able to control her actions, for a time. But I knew I did not have the capacity to control her heart. While I was deeply opposed to her plans, I told her I would continue to care about her, even if she carried them out. I left the conversation disheartened, convinced I had not made my points. I fully expected she would leave home.

But she didn't. While it was obvious that her love for the young man remained strong, at the end of a week it became clear that she was not going to move in with him. I then told her about my feelings at the end of our difficult conversation a week previous. "I really thought you would leave," I confessed. "Why didn't you go?"

"Your arguments weren't very convincing," she said, "but the more we talked, the more I could see how opposed you are to what I want to do, and the more I could feel how much you care about me. You didn't change my mind, but I can't go against your caring."

The point of the story is *not* that I was right and my daughter was wrong—though years later we now agree that her choice not to leave was right for her. Rarely can any of us know absolutely what is best for another. The point is not that I was right but that I now realize my caring reflected more than just my caring. Consider again the dynamics of the incident.

My daughter faces an important decision. She expects me to tell her that I believe that what she wants to do is morally wrong and moreover impractical. Nevertheless she is determined. She knows that I can't control her. I may be able to control her actions temporarily, but she knows I can't control her feelings or her will. In our encounter she experiences not simply my concern but the unconditional nature of my caring. She realizes that I will continue to care whether she acts out what she wants or gives in to what I want for her. Whether she stays or goes (like the son who left home in Jesus' parable of the prodigal son), my caring remains. She recognizes that this caring is more than she expected from me. While she may discount my arguments, she cannot discount this caring.

Now, years later, as I look back at my behavior I marvel at my responses. I recognize that I outdid myself. In truth, I wanted to control her. I thought that what she wanted to do was wrong. If she acted out her proposal, I believed she would jeopardize her future. What possessed me that I was able to resist being moralistic or controlling and to extend this care out of myself that helped her get back in touch with herself? I think God possessed me. I think she and I experienced more than my caring. I think we were touched by the soul power of God; we were blessed. Just an ordinary daughter and father, hardly of outstanding concern in God's economy, but we were blessed.

That blessing brought each of us back to the self God created. To be Christ-like, Carl Jung suggests somewhere, is not to "ape Jesus" but to become that person God created us to be. Just as Jesus in the flesh incarnated and communicated godliness in his humanity, though we cannot perfectly mirror godliness, we can reflect it in and through our humanity. The blessing of God redeemed within me the good self God made. That blessing then moved through me and touched my daughter. Though I fumbled, she felt the care of God and came to herself.

Living by faith becomes a possibility when we believe the good news about God: "The soul power of God is at your fingertips; change your heart and mind and believe this good news." We open ourselves to receive the gifts of God when we live in our daily lives as though the scriptural descriptions of the nature of God's care for us were true—and discover that they are. God is not simply an idea or an ideal; God has character. God's blessing reflects that character. To believe in God in general is possible but hardly meaningful. It's like believing in marriage in general. It's the difference between embracing a concept and embracing someone. It's the difference between being sustained by an idea and being sustained by a faithful lover who will never fail you.

God's Gracious Boundaries

When we open ourselves to God's caring, we discover that God's love includes not only a sustaining center but protective boundaries. We are sustained as we open ourselves to God's love and as we honor the commandments that form a counterpoint. To stay in touch with the benefits of the love, we need to honor the boundaries. The boundaries formed by God's law are as much a manifestation of God grace as God's love is.

I first understood how God's commandments are a manifestation of God's care during a lecture on liturgy. The liturgics professor pointed out that John Calvin placed the Ten Commandments *after* the prayer of confession and the words of assurance in his order of worship in order to highlight them as signs of God's love. In the original version (Ex. 20) they are introduced with a testimony to God's care: "'I am the Lord, your God, who brought you out of the land of Egypt, out of the house of slavery.'" It is as though God says, "I have proved by my actions in your behalf that I care for you. To ensure that you stay in touch with this caring, I give you these commandments." When we fail to honor the boundaries described in the commandments, we endanger our relationship with God and our relationships with one another. Consider the protection the commandments provide:

> You shall have no other gods before me.
> You shall not make for yourself an idol.
> You shall not make wrongful use of the name of the
>   Lord your God.
> Remember the sabbath day, and keep it holy.
> Honor your father and your mother.
> You shall not murder.
> You shall not commit adultery.
> You shall not steal.
> You shall not bear false witness.
> You shall not covet.
>
> —Exodus 20:1–17

These boundaries protect us from jeopardizing our relationship with God, from violating other humans, and from destroying ourselves. Centering our lives on a god of our own making who cannot provide the care God can; trying to use God for less than godly purposes; failing to recognize our need for rest and worship, the key relationship of parents and children, the horrors of killing, and the self-destruction that comes from adultery, stealing, lying, and coveting—all are essential to sustain life.

The commandments are to be taken literally, not, as one friend suggested in jest, as "guidelines." We run grave risks when we fail to honor the boundaries they represent. Though we may not see the hazards at first, they eventually come home to us. Consider, for example, our retreat as a society from the permissiveness of two or three decades ago. In *Frameworks* I described the popularity of the open marriage movement in the late 1960s and early 1970s.[2] Books written by advocates of open marriage describe "intimate friendships," which include sexual intimacy with a variety of persons, as potentially enriching experiences.[3] They imply that those who hold to the old strictures are depriving themselves unnecessarily.

After only a brief spurt of popularity, the open marriage movement lost its appeal. Even those who now choose to live together without marrying live mostly in committed relationships that rarely include "intimate friendships" with others. What happened? Why are more people, even those who do not accept the divine authority of this commandment, honoring it? Largely because it has become apparent that breaking this commandment is not simply wrong but is destructive.

The problem with violating one of these God-given commandments is not simply that I transgress but that I *become* a transgressor. Not only do I steal; I become a thief. Not only do I practice idolatry; I become an idolater. Not only do I commit adultery; I become an adulterer. In each instance something happens to me, something destructive. I become less than what I was, a corruption of what I was.

When we are tempted to violate one of the boundaries God has established, we must turn away (repent) immediately, lest we be destroyed. This concern, that we recognize the danger at the earliest possible moment and turn away, is at the root of Jesus' caution, "'But I say to you that everyone who looks at a woman with lust has already committed adultery with her in his heart' [Matt. 5:28]." Though some are repelled by Jesus' words, his warning is *not* an overstatement. It is simply a description of reality. The look and the act are too easily connected. We must turn away (repent) immediately and break the connection lest we harm the other and ourselves and our relationship with God.

The boundaries God sets in the commandments point up limits we must honor to keep our humanity. They show us how our lives can thrive and how to prevent our lives from breaking down. The counterpoint of the devotion that forms the center of my relationship with my wife, Sherry, is the commitment that forms its boundaries. Sherry and I know it is safe to give ourselves unreservedly to our relationship because we are committed to its boundaries. If either of us finds another person appealing, or if someone challenges either of us to violate our commitment, we do not respond. We do not respond because we have decided ahead of time not to respond. One can be "carried away" only if one is available to be carried away.

The commitment to honor the commandment to "have no other gods before me" is similar to the commitment to honor the promise, "forsaking every other, cleave to her/him only, so long as you both shall live." I can begin the relationship when I decide to honor one, not the others. I can keep the relationship when I decide again to honor one, not the others.

We become the persons God created us to be as we are blessed with God's soul power. That godliness continues in our lives as we embrace God's endless love and honor the boundaries set by God's commandments.

CHAPTER 4

Finding Certainty by Doubting

Jim is dead.

Jim is dead! The phrase keeps repeating itself in my mind as I stand staring into an open grave on this cold, rainy fall day. Jim is dead.

I look at Jim's dad seated in his wheelchair, the tears dripping off of his cheeks on to his parka. As always, he embodies courage. For many years the wheelchair has been his daytime home. Crippling arthritis long ago robbed him of the use of his feet and hands. Though he cannot hold a toothbrush, he has taught his misshapen right hand to operate a Morse code key. Dots and dashes traveling out from his code key and returning through his earphones link him to hundreds of friends he will never be able to visit in person.

The old father's tears express more than the usual grief a parent feels at the loss of a child. Jim's fingers on the piano keyboard gave sound to music his father also heard within. The grand piano in the parlor now stands silent. There are only tape recordings, electronic pictures to which we all cling in a futile effort to recall this living son-friend-artist who now seems forever beyond us.

"It's pretty rotten," I tell myself. "Why should these simple headaches that began only eight months ago expand to a tumor that kills my friend at age thirty-eight?" My anger swells up: "Are you really running things, God?" I crave an answer; and I don't want any sentimental slop.

I feel myself slipping into doubt. "Why pick on this one, God? There are plenty of others who deserve it more than he does." Words from Psalm 73 (vv. 4–5) that describe the unfair and seemingly easy escape of the wicked from adversity are amplified in my head:

> For they have no pain;
>> their bodies are sound and sleek.
> They are not in trouble as others are;
>> they are not plagued like other people.

I crave a present-day answer to an ancient dilemma: Why is life so unfair? Why do so many who seem evil live on while this good man, my best friend, lies in his grave?

Doubt, Believing, and Faith

What happens when we doubt?

What we confront when we doubt differs according to the kind of doubt we experience. There are at least two kinds of doubt: the troublesome doubt that comes to us when our way of believing proves to be inadequate and the more profound doubt that overwhelms us when we truly lose our faith. Losing our way of believing leads to one kind of doubt; losing our faith to another.

When our way of believing breaks down, we experience what I call believing doubt. Such was the doubt that plagued me that day in the cemetery. My model of the way God relates to the world fell apart. The tragic loss of my friend unexpectedly confronted me with some inadequacies in my way of believing. The theological rationale on which I then depended failed me. I did not lose faith in God; I lost faith in the model I was then using to characterize the relationship of God with the world. To recover my believing I was forced to construct a new and more adequate model.

Doubt that causes us to lose our faith is usually more serious than doubt that undermines our way of believing. While losing our way of believing can be frightening, losing our faith can be devastating. I lost my way of understanding how God relates to the world that day in the cemetery, but I did not lose my conviction that

God is deeply involved in the world. Though I was no longer clear about how God is involved, I retained my conviction that all of us are somehow in the hands of God. I lost my way of believing, but I held on to faith in God, and that faith sustained me while I built a new model of believing. Later on in this chapter I will suggest how we can find our way through the despairing doubt that may overwhelm us when we lose our faith. But first, in this section, I want to explore how we can find certainty again when we realize that our ways of believing are inadequate.

Discovering that our ways of believing are no longer adequate is an understandably common experience today. In *Frameworks* I described how the normative framework of beliefs once at the core of American society has been replaced by religious pluralism.[1] When that normative cultural framework was intact most people's constructed belief systems employed similar theological perspectives to describe how God is related to the world. Each person rightly assumed that other people's models would be composed of essentially the same perspectives as his or her own model.

Such an assumption is no longer warranted in today's pluralistic culture. There are few theological perspectives that everyone, or even that most people, share. Many people do not feel obligated to honor the authority of any traditional or church-based way of believing. They feel free to construct their own personal theological models. When viewed from traditional Christian perspectives, many of these models include elements that would have appeared quite unorthodox to our forebearers. As a society we no longer affirm a common, normative theological framework.

Recently one of my sons and I were discussing the situation believers face today. He observed that someone facing doubt now will find there is as much "evidence" available that argues against believing in God as there is that argues for believing in God. Today if doubt overtakes us, more than likely we will have to construct our own models to discover how we can believe again. When some experience like the unjust death of my friend at age thirty-eight challenges our way of believing, we cannot look to a common cultural framework to provide ready-made answers to our doubts. While others may assist, in the final analysis each of us has to discover how he or she can again believe. What can we do?

When we lose only our way of believing, it is important to recognize that we have not lost our faith. Usually we can draw on that faith to sustain us while we discover how we can believe. Recently I read a novel entitled *The Inside of the Cup* by a turn-of-the-century American author named Winston Churchill.[2] Through a series of unnerving incidents the hero of the novel, an Episcopal priest named John Hodder, loses his way of believing. But he does not lose his faith, and when he realizes he still has his faith to hold on to, he recognizes that it can sustain him while he searches for new ways of believing.

> Gradually Hodder was filled with a feeling which may be called amazement because, although his brain was no nearer to a solution than before, he was not despondent. . . . He had feared *reality*. He had insisted upon gazing at the universe through the coloured glasses of an out-worn theology, instead of using his own eyes. . . .
>
> He found himself, to his surprise, surveying with equanimity the pile of books in the corner which had led him to the conviction of the emptiness of the universe— but the universe was no longer empty! It was cruel, but a warring force was at work in it which was not blind, but *directed*. He could not say why this was so, but he *knew* it, he *felt* it, sensed its energy within him. [3]

In the midst of broken believing, Hodder realizes that his faith in God has held. I made the same discovery in the days following my friend's death. As any human is always more than our mental pictures of her or him, so God always exceeds our theology. God is neither contained nor exhausted in our theological models. The mystery of God always turns out to be more profound than the insights that compose our particular certainty.

Faith is beyond belief—beyond any way of believing. When we lose our way of believing, we need not lose our faith. Quite the opposite, we can draw on our faith to sustain us while we discover how we can believe again. To recall the diagram in chapter one: Believing is within us, but faith is between us and God. While we may be confused and anxious when we lose our way of believing, we do not need to lose touch with God when our believing gives way to doubting.

God does not reject us or withdraw when we doubt. In the strength of that realization we can face the doubts that plague us. We can ask our "why" questions boldly. We can doubt as passionately or angrily as we need to. The more open we are with our questions, the more likely we are to resolve them. Open searching encourages us to let go of outmoded believing and to move ahead in our believing. It opens us to new possibilities for believing.

The writer of Psalm 73 discovers new believing through open, passionate questioning. The inspiration that enables this ancient doubter to believe again comes during quiet moments that bring new believing that answers the painful questioning.

> When my soul was embittered,
>   when I was pricked in heart,
> I was stupid and ignorant;
>   I was like a brute beast toward you.
> Nevertheless I am continually with you;
>   you hold my right hand.
> You guide me with your counsel,
>   and afterward you will receive me with honor.
> Whom have I in heaven but you?
>   And there is nothing on earth
>   that I desire other than you.
> My flesh and my heart may fail,
>   but God is the strength of my
>   heart and my portion forever.
> —Psalm 73:21-26

The psalmist's experience reminds me of my own as I stood in the cemetery. When I turned away from the grave, the wind struck me in the face. With the wind came another recollection of scripture: "'The wind blows where it chooses, and you hear the sound of it, but you do not know where it comes from or where it goes. So it is with everyone who is born of the Spirit' [John 3:8]."

The wind drew me beyond the cemetery, beyond my doubt. This incident in my life, the unjust loss of my friend, was still unexplained. I was confused, but I felt solid. To let this unexplained incident undermine the whole of my believing would be foolish. Like the psalmist I realized that such shortsightedness would be "stupid" and "ignorant." I knew I would have to expand my way of believing to account for this tragedy. That would take time; it would not be easy. Though at the moment, I could not see how I could integrate this unjust death into my way of believing, I knew it would happen. And it has.

The Necessity of Doubting

When we cannot account for some experience within our current way of believing, we must expand our way of believing or look for another way of believing. The onset of doubt signals the need to expand or change our believing. Doubt reminds us that there is much about God and about life that we have yet to understand.

Doubt is inevitable and necessary. Doubting is bound up with believing. The need to doubt at some future time is built into every way of believing because any model we construct to characterize God and God's relationship to the creation will sooner or later prove to be inadequate. The onset of doubt tells us we now need to revise or expand our way of believing to find certainty again. The new certainty we then discover includes the potential for doubt in the future. This rhythm of doubt and certainty is a natural dynamic of human believing.

Recognizing that doubt *normally* alternates with believing makes it easier for us to accept doubt as a necessary step to expanded or deeper believing. Recalling that believing has followed doubt in the past can give us the courage we need to plunge into doubting. Each time we make the plunge we become aware again that we believe by building a model to characterize God. And on each new occasion when we discover our present model is inadequate, we realize we need to construct a more adequate way of believing.

Being willing to recognize such inadequacy opens us to new ways of believing. We are able to consider new or different evidence. As I noted, the writer of Psalm 73 discovers new believing through such open questioning. So did I when I turned away from Jim's grave that day in the cemetery. The wind moved me to look beyond my doubting to consider new approaches that could expand my believing.

When we realize that doubt and believing form an essential rhythm that brings us again and again to certainty, we welcome doubt as a prelude to expanded believing. Doubt reminds us that God's ways are always to some degree beyond our believing. Doubt pushes us to reach beyond our grasp, to look beyond the borders of our current beliefs, to crane our theological necks to peer around the corners of our current believing.

When my friend died I was forced to recognize that I had included in my model of God's relationship to the world the simplistic assumption that God's involvement should result in life being fair. The model I employed to characterize God's involvement was similar to a cosmic household in which the parent (God) controls the children *and makes certain* that each receives fair treatment. Such, I discovered, is not the case. I now realize that most of us encounter experiences during the course of living that can cause us to question whether life in this world, whatever the nature of God's involvement, is fair.

For many of us the discovery is triggered by an unforgetable incident. I recall a conversation some years ago with a man whose way of believing was shattered by the accidental death of his eleven-year-old son. The boy went off one morning to a nearby river to fish. He slipped on a rock, hit his head, fell into the river, and drowned. A companion, who might have prevented the tragedy, panicked. Instead of rushing to the closest house for help, he ran three-quarters of a mile, all the way to the boy's home, to tell the boy's father of the accident. When the father ran back to the river, it was too late.

"Every day, up until that day, I prayed to God to take care of my family," the father told me. "But it doesn't work. I won't say I don't believe in God; but I'll never trust God again."

Our conversation occurred ten years after the accident. Though a decade had elapsed, this man's doubting continued to immobilize his believing. He could not and would not move on. Looking back on his response to his son's death and mine to my friend's death, I realize that he and I were both handicapped by a kind of hothouse believing, believing that requires a protected and regulated environment to survive. We both discovered with a jolt that our hothouse believing withered in the heat of daily living.

Doubt comes to all of us, sometimes as the result of a sudden, unexpected experience and sometimes as the outcome of a slow crumbling of our way of believing. Scripture records women's and men's struggle to believe in the face of doubt. Their experiences resemble the struggles of present-day women and men around us. The life stories of both ancient and modern believers show us that doubt is a reality that all honest believers face. Their experiences offer suggestions that we may be able to follow as we contend with our own doubts. What clues do they offer?

1. Regardless of how doubt arrives, *those who find a way to believe again do so because they keep moving and searching in spite of their doubt.* They accept the reality of doubt, face up to it, and move on, assuming they will discover how they can believe again. And they do. They discover how to rebuild their believing because they do not permit doubt to immobilize them.

Not long ago I talked with a woman whose husband has suffered from a debilitating disease for several years. I found myself wondering how she could continue to believe in God's care as she watched the painfully slow wasting of his body and mind.

"Don't you sometimes wonder how God can let something like this happen?" I wanted to ask her.

Somehow, I think, she sensed what I was thinking. She squelched my question before I could ask it. She said: "Sometimes I wonder at the strength that continues to well up in me as I care for him day after day."

This woman's experience challenged me to expand my way of believing. I discovered I was focusing on a fruitless rather than a fruitful question. Her believing challenged me to give up my fruitless wondering; she showed me by her ongoing life that there is a universal source of strength on which we can draw when we are caught in adversity. How much greater is the certainty I received from her than the doubt I brought to her. Now when adversity comes into my life I am usually able to bypass the unanswerable Why-does-this-happen? question and immediately reach out to God to seek the strength I need to walk on. From this woman, and others like her, I have learned to keep moving when I doubt. I search expectantly, and sooner or later I discover how I can believe again.

2. *Refusing to doubt can handicap our believing; it may make our believing dangerous to others.* Refusing to open our believing to the scrutiny of doubt makes us vulnerable to self-deception. This self-deception can have serious consequences.

Several years ago in a town not far away from where I live, a young man on a hunting expedition accidentally shot and killed his companion. A local minister interpreted the accident to him as not accidental at all. He described the shooting as an act of God.

"You didn't pull that trigger," he told the young man. "God's hand was on top of yours. God wanted your friend to be in heaven with him. God's hand worked inside yours to pull the trigger. You were just God's servant, doing God's will. Your friend is better off than we are now because he is with God."

When something happens that we cannot explain, we may be tempted to preserve our way of believing by forcing God to fit into our model. Avoiding doubt in that way sometimes encourages us to hold on to a distorted picture of God, which we may then impose on others. Those who hold such a distorted picture and seek to impose it on others can be dangerous. It is sad to review the record of evil perpetrated in the name of God by those who refuse to doubt. The list stretches from the Roman Catholic Inquisition in Spain to the Reformation Church in Geneva, from the Reformed Church in South Africa to the local Independent Bible Church minister in the town next to me.

Doubt is as deeply ingrained in our humanity as sin; in fact, they work similarly in our lives. When I was a theological student, Dr. MacLean, my Old Testament professor, taught me that the imagery surrounding the Hebrew word for "sin" is based on archery. It calls forth the image of a bowman trying again and again to hit a target but always missing it. He wants to hit it, but he cannot. This understanding of sin implies that we are inherently flawed. However well-intentioned we may be, we can never be perfect. The problem is not that we don't try but that we always, to a greater or lesser extent, miss being godly. (Recall St. Paul's similarly poignant description of the human condition in Romans 7.)

Our believing is never perfect. Because we are sinful persons, our believing is always to some degree flawed. Doubting, like confessing, is necessary to our and others' well-being. Doubting that leads us to question outmoded or erroneous or dangerous believing is essential. A person who refuses to doubt can be as great a hazard as a person who refuses to own up to sin.

When We Truly Lose Our Faith

To lose our faith is a much deeper, more threatening experience than to lose our way of believing. Doubt that comes over us when we lose our way of believing often leads to anxiety; doubt that overcomes us when we lose our faith often results in despair. When doubt challenges our way of believing, God seems hidden; we are anxious and confused. When doubt undermines our faith, we feel God cannot help us; God seems unreachable, impotent.

In chapter 11 verses 32–44 of his Gospel, John describes a family who are filled with despairing doubt. Jesus journeys to Bethany to visit Mary, Martha, and Lazarus, their brother, and discovers that Lazarus died four days before his arrival. We feel Mary's and Martha's hopelessness in their conversation with Jesus. You are too late, Mary tells him; her brother is beyond help.

"Lord, if you had been here, my brother would not have died," Mary says.

"Where have you laid him?" Jesus asks.

They reply: "Lord, come and see." Even Jesus is overcome by their grieving, and weeps.

Recovering, Jesus directs them to remove the stone that covers the opening to Lazarus' tomb. But they see no point in doing so; Lazarus is beyond help. "Lord, already there is a stench because he has been dead four days."

Something more than a way of believing has been lost here. Lazarus' family and friends feel powerless. Lazarus is dead. There is nothing they can do. Within their own resources, there is no remedy.

When we feel ourselves overcome by doubt that undermines our faith, we realize how much more serious it is to lose our faith than it is to lose our way of believing. Believing is essentially a human activity. We build belief models over and over again, each time redrawing our picture of the way God relates to us and to the world. Each redrawing addresses challenges we have encountered since the previous redrawing.

When we lose our faith, we lose our ability to develop a new model of believing. We doubt ourselves, and, what is even more serious, we doubt God. We are immobilized. Like Martha and Mary, we doubt that God can (or will) help us.

When we truly lose our faith, only God can help us. To recognize that faith is what we have lost, not simply our way of believing, and that faith comes to us only as a gift from God is extremely important. It shifts the focus of attention away from what we might struggle in vain to accomplish toward what God can and will give us. If we can bring ourselves to reach out, help is available. The Christian gospel is plain: God wants to help us; God will help us. The heart of the Christian faith is a promise: we can count on God. God has initiated, already is initiating, and always will initiate the relationship that makes faith possible.

In his response to Lazarus' death, Jesus turns the promise into present reality. He responds to Martha's matter-of-fact statement that Lazarus has been dead four days with a matter-of-fact statement of his own, "'Did I not tell you that if you believed you would see the glory of God?'" ("Glory" here means the essence or reality of God.) Then John tells us, "They took away the stone." Jesus prays to God and calls out to Lazarus, and the man who was dead four days walks out of the tomb. God does what no person was able to do.

We see the key to their recovery—their willingness to reach out—in the simple statement: "They took away the stone." They struggle to find a way through their doubt, to bring themselves to reach out. That reaching out begins in their willingness to bring *whatever they feel and press that on God.* The two sisters press their hopelessness on Jesus. They insist that he deal with what they feel. They prod him with their despairing doubt. This willingness to push themselves forward with their doubt and all that stems from that doubt, to push their doubt at God, makes them available to receive the grace that in the end revitalizes their faith.

The fatal mistake of doubting is to imagine we are unacceptable to God when we doubt. Doubting is not a moral issue. By itself it is not sin; it is not sinful. Whatever we may feel along with the doubt, we are *never* unacceptable to God because we doubt. Thomas, the classic doubter of scripture, despairing over the loss of Jesus in whom he had invested all his hopes, brings his doubt to God in the form of an angry challenge. When the other disciples tell Thomas they have seen the risen Christ, he responds with cynical, challenging doubt, "'Unless I see the mark of the nails in his hands, and put my finger in the mark of the nails and my hand in his side, I will not believe' [John 20:25]."

Jesus takes Thomas' statement at face value. Jesus' response is a clear testimony to the depth of God's willingness to do whatever is needed to revive faith in us. Jesus comes to Thomas and says, "'Put your finger here and see my hands. Reach out your hand and put it in my side. Do not doubt but believe' [John 20:27]."

If we make ourselves available and permit God to act in our lives, God will do whatever needs to be done to enable us to recover our faith. Usually that process of revitalization begins when we identify what is blocking us from receiving the faith-enlivening grace of God and, like Thomas, face God directly with the source of our doubt. It may take some time before we are able to present ourselves to God with the doubt that paralyzes us.

Some years before the death of my friend Jim, I went through several months of deep doubt and depression. A good friend had committed suicide. One of my children developed a destructive illness from which she has never recovered. The ministry in which I was engaged seemed to be going nowhere. As the days went by during that winter, I felt my faith slipping away. I kept going through the motions, maintaining my spiritual discipline. But my prayers seemed to accomplish nothing. In late January I caught a cold that developed into virus pneumonia. My body did not respond to the medicine my doctor prescribed; my condition worsened even after a month of treatment. Each day during that month my physician, a member of the congregation I served and a good friend, came to my home every morning and evening to give me an injection of antibiotics. One February evening, after giving me the injection, he sat next to me on the bed, looked into my eyes, and asked, "What's wrong?"

I remember being speechless. Tears flowed down my cheeks. I couldn't say what specifically was at the root of the maladies I experienced; everything seemed wrong. His concern may have helped to turn the tide. Whatever the reason, the medicine began to work. I recovered enough strength to begin to work. But God still seemed distant, like a character in my childhood. And I was now struggling to live as an adult in what seemed like a God-forsaken world.

In the late spring I had to make a trip to a large city. One afternoon when I was free for a few hours I went for a walk and came upon a large Roman Catholic church. Something drew me inside. I sat down in a pew at the back of the sanctuary. No one else was there.

Then there was Someone there. At the same time that I felt that Presence, I felt all the frightening doubt well up within me. I was overcome by it. I cried out, "God!" I heard my cry echo throughout the church.

Then all was quiet. I realized I also was quiet—for the first time in many months. I had no doubt of the source of the peace I felt. This peace was not simply the result of some psychological release.

I later understood the source of the psychological stress that compounded my doubt. As a Christian and as a minister, I thought others were depending on me to be a person of faith. I mistakenly thought that a true person of faith does not have serious doubts. For months I had been hiding the nagging, doubting side of myself from God. That deception slowly built distance between me and God. As the distance increased my doubt worsened; more and more I lost contact with God. Increasingly cut off from God, I lost touch with the re-sources of grace that could have helped me cope with individual, difficult experiences in my life as they oc-curred. Instead, each new challenge became a crisis that increased my doubt, further alienating me from God.

Eventually I became so alienated that my spirit could not receive the benefits of God's healing grace any more than my body could receive the healing benefits of the antibiotics the doctor was injecting.

When I cried out "God!" in the sanctuary and let my pent-up emotions burst forth, my soul burst forth as well. The peace that then came to me was beyond my understanding. It healed me in ways I did not then understand.

In our highly cerebral culture we are likely to make faith a basically rational matter. But faith is rooted in God, who is beyond our rational believing. Faith differs from believing. Faith is relational, not conceptual. When something blocks our relationship with God, we lose touch with God. In much the same way as we are not free to receive or enjoy the love and care a spouse wants to give us when we are alienated from that spouse, when we are alienated from God, we are not able to receive and enjoy some of the gifts and benefits that would normally come to us from God. Each day our doubt continues we struggle harder to live with the feelings and shortcomings that stem from it. The struggle is all the more painful because we are usually still aware of what the other used to give us and of how much more difficult life is for us without it.

As I suggested earlier in this chapter, doubt resembles sin in its ability to alienate us from God. When we own up to our despair and alienation and hunger and bring whatever we feel to God, we give God a chance to reach out to us. When we cry out, "God!"—God responds. What we perceive in that response is care, not clarity. Like a faithful spouse, God loves us. The peace we receive in faith exceeds our understanding. In the strength of grace we recover our certainty. With faith solid again we are eventually able to rebuild our way of believing.

The great medieval mystics, who invested themselves in life-long efforts to understand how we can maintain openness to God's grace, often wrote of our need to

"practice the presence of God." Tending to spiritual formation and maintaining spiritual discipline seem even
more essential in our world than they were in theirs. All
relationships, including a relationship with God, now
seem more difficult to build and maintain. Many of us
struggle to keep in touch and to keep ourselves together
as we travel rapidly through the often alienated segments
that compose the disconnected worlds in which we live.
It seems essential to me to conclude this book on the
dynamics of believing with a chapter suggesting a framework of spiritual discipline that can nurture our believing and help us to stay open to the gift of faith.

CHAPTER 5

Living out of Receiving into Giving

Before dawn I am awakened by the persistent rapping of a state police officer at my door. He apologizes for the intrusion and then shares his tragic news. Some time during the night Fred, a member of the congregation, ran his car off the road, struck a tree, and was killed. Apparently he fell asleep, the officer suggests. He was alone. No liquor was involved. In fact, the car was full of Easter candy and toys.

It is not difficult to put the pieces together. Unable to find work locally, Fred reluctantly became a long-haul trucker. Though the pay was good, he hated the days away from home. He pushed to complete each run quickly so he could spend as much time as possible at home with his wife and children. Arriving back at the truck terminal late this Saturday night before Easter, he transferred the presents he had purchased for his children from the truck cab to his car and began the fifty-mile drive home. Fatigue proved too much for him. Just ten miles short of his goal he fell asleep. A few hundred feet later his life ended when his car hit an oak tree.

The police officer asks me to go with him to break the news to Sally, Fred's wife. "They're my friends," he says, "I just can't take that candy and those presents to her by myself." So, Easter begins with a 4 A.M. ride to share a tragedy. Somehow I make my way through the worship services later that morning. Easter night I go with Sally to choose a casket. I am back to stand with her at the calling hours Monday and to conduct the funeral service on Tuesday. Knowing her friends and family will return to their own homes after a day or two, I visit her and the children Friday morning. Now that everyone is gone, she lets herself get angry. I sit with her while she rails at the "rotten God" who took her husband away—and while that same God fills her with healing grace.

As I drive back to my office, I am suddenly overcome with weariness. I try to work on the sermon for the coming Sunday—to no avail. I simply don't have the energy. After lunch I decide to take a break and plant the seeds I had originally planned to sow Easter Monday. Worn out and preoccupied, I do not notice John, a neighbor and member of my church board, until he speaks.

"What are you doing?" he asks.

"Hi, John," I reply, surprised to see him standing over me. "I usually work on Friday. As you know, Monday is my day off. But this has been quite a week! On top of the usual visits, I've spent endless hours with Fred's family. I know I really ought to be working on my sermon. But I can't seem to make myself write. I thought if maybe I stole a few hours of time, I might then be able to get somewhere on it."

"Whoa!" he says before I can start another sentence. "I didn't want an explanation. I just wanted to know what you were planting. I've watched ministers garden on this plot for thirty years, and I can tell you which vegetables usually do better on this end of it. I already know how hard you've been working."

His remarks stood me up straight. Why was I explaining?

The Hazards of Giving

Already in with my childhood and later in my adult life, the Christians I knew seemed always to describe being a faithful Christian exclusively in terms of giving, never receiving. While I knew that God cares for me, that knowledge was confined to my head. My day-to-day experiential relationship with God was almost exclusively a matter of what I thought I should do for God. I struggled with how I should serve God, how I "ought" to give of myself, what I ought to do to show that I am faithful.

When I felt called to become a minister, I naturally believed that becoming a minister meant mostly learning how to do a minister's work. Those who encouraged me to be a minister talked about how much good I could do in that role. Those who prepared me for ministry taught me how to give myself in ministry. Hardly anyone showed me or encouraged me to learn how to receive the grace I (and all of us) need to become and survive as a Christian person. Even the meager attention given to spiritual formation during my preparation related it to the work of ministry. I learned to pray better in order to be able to give more.

That subtle connecting of prayer to work took hold firmly during the early years of my ministry. Following the model of ministry presented to me at seminary, I scheduled a time for personal devotions into the work day. But as I read scripture I found myself mostly writing notes in my journal that would become sermons. In my praying I found myself mostly focusing on the needs of my congregation and community and on what I should do to respond to these needs. My Christian identity became increasingly dependent on my work. By scheduling my personal devotions into my work time, even my praying became work related. My personal piety was part of my work.

Once the pattern was set, working harder to feel more spiritual was a natural outcome. I had a clear sense of being Christian only as I did ministry. Even when exhaustion overcame me, as it did when I found myself unable to write a sermon that Friday after Easter, I found it difficult to feel godly when I took time off. The language I used to think about time off, that I was "taking" it, as though it were time stolen from the work of ministry, undermined my capacity to feel godly when I was apart from work. And when church members like

John found me not working, I felt called to explain to them why I was not working, lest they see me as not a faithful Christian.

Looking back on the first three decades of my life, I realize I took to heart the definition of Christian living that is most common in work-oriented American culture. In an insightful pamphlet he wrote almost ten years ago, Carl Dudley makes a helpful distinction between what he calls "rigorous" and "relational" orientations to believing.

> [Rigorous believers] begin by contributing. . . . Faith begins when the believer qualifies by acknowledging his or her need for God, and promises to will one will with the Divine. (Obligation precedes gospel.) . . . Urgency is natural for rigorous faith. . . . Improvement is the bottom line for the believer with rigorous faith. . . . Individual effort and tireless productivity provide evidence that faith is genuine.
>
> [Relational believers] begin with belonging. . . . Faith is discovered within a believing community, symbolized by infant baptism. (Gospel-love precedes obligation.) . . . People become closer, holding hands, embracing, sharing stories, and relaxing together. They heal each other by touching, from the friendly greeting to the formal laying on of hands. The outside world may be evil, but within the group they feel reassured, renewed. When one of the members needs help, the response is often overwhelming. They care deeply, respond fully.[1]

Dudley goes on to assert that a wholesome, rounded approach to believing embraces both orientations. The dominant values of our culture, however, encourage us to recognize only action-oriented faith as legitimate. As a result, many of us have learned only rigorous ways of believing. The consequences are unfortunate: we are much better at giving than we are at receiving. Many of us have never learned how to receive the essential nurture we need to keep on giving.

Several years ago a new professor of counseling who was being inaugurated at his university decided to include a demonstration within his inaugural address. He invited those present to participate in a role play designed to illustrate how counseling can be helpful. After explaining the purpose of the demonstration, he asked for a volunteer to act as the counselor. Nearly one hundred of his colleagues raised their hands. Then the professor asked for a volunteer to describe a problem with which he or she needed help. *No one responded!* He assured those gathered that even an invented illustration would do. Only after repeated invitations was he able to convince a student member of the audience to share a problem. More than one hundred colleagues were willing to be identified as givers; not one was willing to be identified publicly as a receiver.

Sherry and I often encounter similar resistance when we work as planning consultants with local church leaders. So long as we focus on what their congregation can give to others, leaders are usually able to participate well. But if we ask them to identify what *they* need to receive from their church, they often become uncomfortable. Most are unable or unwilling to see themselves (or let themselves be seen) as receivers.

I think Carl Dudley is correct: a holistic way of believing includes both rigorous and relational elements. We will not thrive if we affirm only rigorous approaches to believing as legitimate. We need relationships with God and others through which we receive sustaining grace to maintain an activist faith. When I am with those who affirm only a rigorous approach to believing as valid, they often seem to me to show evidence of their deprivation. Recently I led a workshop for just such a group. They were hardened, worn-down, driven, joyless people. I empathized with them because I once could accept only rigorous believing as legitimate. I, too, was once a hardened, driven, worn-down, and joyless believer. Several confrontations like the one with my neighbor, John, and, most of all, some pointed counseling from a deeply spiritual and very competent psychotherapist helped me to accept rigorous and relational aspects of believing as equally legitimate and necessary. It may be more blessed to give than to receive; but one who cannot receive soon finds it difficult to keep giving.

Even Jesus found it necessary to receive.   A close reading of the Gospels reveals that he regularly withdrew from the often frenzied activity of his life to pray and to draw sustenance from his disciples and friends.   One cannot read the story of his earthly life without realizing how much friends such as Mary, Martha, and Lazarus and disciples such as Peter, James, and John meant to him.   We catch the significance they held for him when he says, "'You are those who have stood by me in my trials' [Luke 22:28]." With Jesus, discipleship and friendship are interrelated.   He makes the essential interdependence of rigorous and relational believing clear to the first disciples when he describes the nature of their relationship with him not as servants to a master but as friends.   "'I do not call you servants any longer . . . but I have called you friends' [John 15:15]."   Jesus invited disciples to receive as well as to give.

A New Responsibility: Spiritual Formation

Voters in the state of Maine, where I live, recently passed a referendum rescinding the state's blue laws. All stores may now open for business on Sundays, and I imagine that most stores will take advantage of this additional opportunity to sell their merchandise.   The action taken by Maine's voters represents more than the right to do business on Sundays.   It removes the last legal reminder of a rhythm that once regulated our American society.   Weekends that give us two days to do what we want to do have replaced prescribed days of rest.   The popular refrain, "Thank God, it's Friday!" is now more commonly heard among us than the commandment, "Remember the sabbath day to keep it holy."

In his article on social change in the small town of New Concord, Ohio, John Baskin describes a symbolic collision between someone who represents the new weekender values and someone who upholds Sabbatarian views.

> On this particular Sunday, the librarian, Grace McClenahan, looked out her window and saw her new neigh-

bor, the highway patrolman, come out to work on his house. She went over.

"This will not do," she said. And by that, she meant the disreputable occurrence of work on the Sabbath. Neither work *nor* play were [sic.] to occur on her Sundays. The New Concord grocer, as a boy, was not allowed to ride his tricycle, and the undertaker's mother recalled being whipped for sitting behind the stove on Sunday reading the almanac. *Work?*

"Have a beer, Miz McClenahan," the patrolman said, "and let's discuss this."[2]

What the demise of the Sabbath points up is worth discussing. Likely it is good to be free of the oppressive ways that were sometimes associated with the old Sabbath ritual. But the waning of the Sabbath is indicative of a basic transition that reaches far beyond the loss of an enforced day of rest. The old religious rituals that once pervaded American society provided a nurturing discipline, not just some oppressive rules. Sabbath observance was one aspect of an overall, normative, religious framework. The regulating force of this framework touched every dimension of life. While we are now free of the oppressive aspects of the old framework, we are also without the benefit of the overarching, regulating rhythm it provided. Few of us have Miz McClenahans to call us to account in the various aspects of our lives, and few would feel compelled to heed her advice should she challenge our lack of spiritual discipline. Each of us must now design and develop a self-regulating discipline of our own. We must now provide our own rhythm that insures nurture as well as action, receiving as well as giving in our lives.

I think the growing concern about spiritual formation in some sections of our society reflects the loss of the old, normative religious framework. Increasingly we become aware that this loss gives each of us the responsibility to develop his or her own spiritual discipline. Though many of us welcome the opportunity to shape our own spiritual formation, few of us are clear about the elements that need to be included. What are the necessary components of an adequate spiritual discipline?

One day a lawyer asked Jesus,

> "What must I do to inherit eternal life?" He said to
> him, "What is written in the law? What do you read
> there?" He answered, "You shall love the Lord your God
> with all your heart, and with all your soul, and with all
> your strength, and with all your mind; and your neighbor
> as yourself." And he [Jesus] said to him, "You have given
> the right answer; do this, and you will live."
>
> —Luke 10:25-28

I believe these four ways of loving God—with heart, soul, strength, and mind—suggest a framework of spiritual discipline. It is clear from the rest of this passage of scripture that loving God involves us immediately in loving our neighbor. Jesus illustrates how loving God is inextricably bound up with loving our neighbor when he goes on in this passage of scripture to tell the story of the Good Samaritan (Luke 10:29-37). Our relationship with God is nurtured and demonstrated in our relationships with other people. By loving God *and* loving others with our heart, soul, strength, and mind, we discipline our believing within a framework of Christian faith.

Giving and receiving are also interconnected in each aspect of loving. As an old adage suggests, "We become what we think about." We become what we give our minds to. And we become what we give our hearts to, and our souls and our strength, as well. We are shaped by those to whom we give our hearts and with whom we invest our souls and minds and strength. Insofar as they are godly people, God reaches through them to mold us.

A Framework of Spiritual Formation

In the closing pages of this book I want to explore the interrelationship between giving and receiving within the context of these four ways of loving that Jesus affirms. Though each way of loving includes both giving and receiving, in this discussion of spiritual formation I think it will be most helpful to concentrate on how we are molded by our giving when we love with all our strength, and how we are molded by what we receive when we love with all our hearts and souls and minds.

Loving with All Our Strength

We love God with all our strength when we *commit* our strength to direct, caring action for our brothers, sisters, and neighbors. "Commitment" is the word I purposely choose to describe what we do. To commit our strength to others means we obligate ourselves to them by our actions. We intentionally place ourselves in positions where they can draw on our strength. We become directly involved with them.

Directly involved means locally involved. I think it is essential to commit ourselves to ministries of caring that are *specific* and *local*. While I certainly believe we all are called to affirm the global reality of the church, I feel local commitments to specific ministry are indispensable. All of us need be involved in *direct acts* of caring for those close to us. Ministries that others carry out in our behalf are no substitute for direct caring we do ourselves.

Affirming only global perspectives in the church can encourage a bureaucratic understanding of ministry. As I travel around the country working with local congregations, I make it a point to read the printed material on their bulletin boards. Regardless of denomination, in nearly every church I see a very one-sided message: local church members should fulfill their obligation to act by *supporting* ministries that others actually carry out. Most of the denominational literature our local church receives to post on our bulletin board describes ministries our congregation should support elsewhere. Unfortunately many local churches and their members have accepted this one-sided message. They view themselves primarily as contributing units who support the mission of the larger church.

Corporate action in our behalf is different from personal and local action we take ourselves. It is too easy to retreat into the protective role of bureaucratic Christians in a bureaucratic church. We are then separated by distance and organization from those to whom we minister. We need to use our imagination to feel them.

To reiterate: I do not want to argue against our need to gain a global perspective and to respond with global commitments. However, both for our spiritual well-being and to be faithful Christians, I believe that each of us needs local commitments that obligate us to *direct and ongoing acts* of ministry. We need to *feel* our strength being challenged as we serve. We need local commitments that make us vulnerable. We need to be available to be touched by someone who says, "I am hungry (or have no place to live or am being abused or . . .) and I need *you* to help me."

It is too easy to become critical of the way others minister when we are not directly involved in local ministry ourselves. Recently someone in my community became highly critical of what he called "the lack of financial responsibility" of those who live in a low income housing project our congregation helped to rehabilitate. Our pastor challenged him to become directly involved in this ministry. He accepted the challenge and was assigned to the committee that works with tenants who are behind in their rent. After a month of direct contact with these tenants, he apologized for his former attitude. "I don't know how some of those people can make it at all with the meager resources they have." When he came into direct contact with those in need and they challenged him to love them with all his strength, he became responsive and responsible. We *are* shaped by what we do.

There is no substitute for being in touch. To love God with all our strength is to seek commitments to ministry that challenge our strength. We declare ourselves. We become vulnerable. We permit others to gain access to our lives. We obligate ourselves. We love with all our strength and we are shaped by that loving.

Loving with All Our Heart

Loving with all our strength is costly. It drains us. Learning how to renew our strength by reaching out to God and others with open hearts is no longer optional. We either learn how to receive or risk becoming hardened and joyless persons.

When we invest our hearts with a particular group of God's people, we are likely to discover, as those first disciples did, that we receive more than a hundredfold in return. My work with students assigned as residents with congregations scattered throughout Maine and the work Sherry and I do together often take us away from our own congregation on Sundays. This past Sunday we worshiped for the first time in several weeks with the small congregation where we are members. As we drove home after the service, we talked about how much we miss the nurture we receive from this congregation when we are away. We know our congregation would not necessarily seem better to those who are members of other congregations, but it nurtures us in ways that no other church does. It is truly our "home" church. Being there is like being home. We committed our hearts to this congregation, and we already have received much more from them than we have given to them.

Recently I asked Scott Planting, my pastor, to speak at an occasion at which I was to be honored. In his remarks he told those gathered that he had asked the members of our congregation's governing board to describe me. One member, Evelyn, who is also my neighbor, said, "Doug is common."

The members of my home congregation know I am common. I am free to be one of the "characters" in this church. I don't have to pretend. They know and accept my weaknesses as well as my strengths. They benefit from me and they put up with me.

I think all of us need a congregation where we share in the common duties of congregational life. Loving with our hearts is often expressed in simple ways. I am often surprised to discover how much the ordinary activities of congregational life nurture me. I look forward to sharing with others at the coffee hour that follows our worship service, to helping cook the food for the Sunday School breakfast, and to helping set up or clear the tables after a church supper. I knew I really had been accepted by the members of this small church when the chair of the women's group asked me to stand at the door to collect the money at the fall supper. I felt greatly honored.

Originally I was attracted to this congregation by the opportunity to participate in its vital ministries to those who lack adequate housing or who are victims of abuse or who struggle with chemical dependency. But as I give myself in service with this group (and elsewhere in my life), I more and more become aware of my need to receive their nurture in the common life we share together. They give to me and I accept my need to receive grace at their hands.

I more and more appreciate the balance Jesus strikes between giving and receiving in his life together with the twelve disciples. When Peter refuses to let Jesus wash his feet, I now know why Jesus challenges him with the statement: "'Unless I wash you, you have no share with me' [John 13:8]." Like Peter, most of us are not as strong or independent as we pretend to be. But, as I suggested earlier in this chapter, we have been acculturated to think we should be, that we should not have to receive. To counteract this acculturation, most of us need to commit ourselves to specific relationships in which we are held accountable to receive, as well as specific relationships in which we are held accountable to give. To quote my neighbor again, we are all "common."

By placing ourselves in a particular congregation we make ourselves vulnerable to receive the grace of God through their ministry. By recognizing that we are common we admit our need to receive as much as to give. By letting someone pour coffee for us, or serve us a plate of food at a ham supper, we open our hearts to receive God's grace from that person. There is very little distance between the bread on the plate at the ham supper and the bread on the plate at the eucharist; both are the Bread of Life. My neighbor, Evelyn, who passes bread to me at the church supper, and at the time of Holy Communion, is mediating the gifts of God to me, on both occasions.

Our capacity to receive the deep care we sometimes need from someone is nurtured when we receive ordinary care from that person. We learn about others and they learn about us in the ordinary exchanges that come about as we live together in a congregation. They learn how to give to us and we to them, and they learn how to receive from us and we from them. When a crisis comes, we each know how to go about giving and receiving. Scott, who held our trembling hands and prayed with us at our table the night our son's wife was killed, is the same Scott with whom we often share a meal, or a concern, or a funny story, or an interesting book. He gave with all his heart that night, as did others in our congregation during the days and weeks that followed. But strange as it may sound, while his and their giving during that difficult time in our lives might appear extraordinary to others, it seemed ordinary to us. It was simply an extension of the ordinary care they give all the time, as we realized again this past Sunday. They know how to love us with all their hearts, and by admitting we are common we allow them into our hearts. The godly care we receive through them enables us to continue giving.

Loving with All Our Mind

To love God with our mind is to commit our believing to God. The dynamics of human believing have been the major focus of this book. Throughout it, I have sought to describe how we become responsible and responsive believers—and what we receive when we do.

Simple faith is not always enviable. The thousand who followed Jim Jones to their deaths at Jonestown had simple faith. What they lacked was critical believing. To love God with our mind is to believe critically. Critical believing, as I have suggested, is sometimes frightening and always involves hard work. As Sir Joshua Reynolds observed, there is nothing a person will not do to avoid the labor of thinking.

It is sad to be with someone who limps through life handicapped with immature, simplistic believing. The anti-intellectualism that is common among some groups of Christians is unfortunate. Critical believing is much more likely to strengthen our capacity to receive faith than to weaken it. The new ways of believing that replace the old ways are likely to lead to more, not less, responsible living.

My experience indicates that we strengthen our believing and thus our capacity to receive faith when we commit our minds to specific areas of exploration and to regular interaction with those who are capable of challenging us. Some of us will find one of these avenues easier to follow than the other. Perhaps because for most of my childhood I was an only child I learned very early how to pursue interests on my own. This natural inclination has made it easy for me to discipline the spiritual formation of my mind. For example, I have explored the nature of the relationship of Jesus with disciples for many years, both by studying scripture and by reading the works of others on this subject. For more than a decade I have tried to clarify the nature of human believing and the relationship between human believing and the faith God gives.

I have several friends who sometimes suggest books or tell me about resources that relate to these areas to which I am committed. Once we are clear about a focus, we are more likely to recognize and gather insights that help us grow in understanding. Others who are aware of our interest know what to share with us.

I willingly submit the fruits of my thinking to the scrutiny of others. I participate in ongoing conversations with those who are capable of challenging me. I often

share my thoughts, including the questions that puzzle
me, with those who are interested and capable of criticiz-
ing me, including my wife, my children, and my friends
and colleagues.   Recently one of my sons married a
woman who is preparing for the ministry.   She is a
warm, caring person, as well as an excellent critic.   She
has already challenged my thinking on several occasions,
much to my benefit.

In American society it is customary to avoid the
subject of religion, or, if it comes up in conversation, to
avoid saying anything critical about another's beliefs.   To
receive criticism in such an atmosphere, we will usually
have to invite it.   To be faithful, we need to seek challenges to our believing.   When we love God with our
mind, we bring the best of our thinking to our believing.
We open our believing to the enabling criticism of others.
We accept their challenges as gifts of grace.   We love God
with our mind.

Loving with All Our Soul

If faith is a gift, to enjoy faith we must be willing and
able to receive it.   As I suggest in both *Frameworks* and
Options, ours does not seem to me to be a society that
encourages ways of believing that prepare us to receive
faith.   To experience God in all of life is counter to the
mainstream culture in which we live.

To know the presence of God within, in our souls, as
we live day by day, we need to "practice the presence of
God," to borrow a phrase from Brother Lawrence, a
seventeenth-century French friar who spent a good part
of his life working in the kitchen of his monastery.   Loving God with our soul, with the core of our being, means
being open to let God shape our inner self.   It involves
building a relationship with God.

Someone once observed that "a relationship is as rich
as its rituals."   Rituals provide a framework that nurtures a relationship.   I am aware of the vital role rituals
play in the relationship Sherry and I share.   We always

hold hands when we pray, both when we are alone, for example, as we give thanks before we eat, and when we are with others, for example, when we participate in the prayers of the people at a public worship service. When I serve the food at a home meal, I always serve her first. When I am writing, she protects me from unnecessary interruptions. These rituals and dozens of others provide a structure that enriches our relationship.

Ritual can provide a structure that helps us practice the presence of God. Nearly twenty-five years ago a good friend gave me a copy of the spiritual letters of Dom John Chapman. In a letter dated April 11, 1927, he writes:

> The only way to pray is to pray; and the way to pray well is to pray much. If one has no time for this, then one must at least pray regularly. But the less one prays, the worse it goes. And if circumstances do not permit even regularity, then one must put up with the fact that when one does try to pray, one can't pray—and our prayer will probably consist of telling this to God.[3]

Spiritual depth comes out of practiced devotion. Rituals are the structural framework of practiced devotion. Thus Chapman's suggestion, "the only way to pray is to pray." The fact that one prays regularly is at least as important as how one prays. Each of us needs to follow rituals that keep our soul open to God's molding.

Most of us will find that we benefit from personal rituals and shared rituals. The personal rituals we develop to help us practice the presence of God can reflect our individual, unique needs and characteristics. Experience has taught me that I need to *schedule* time to open my soul to God and that I need to be alone during some of this time. I've discovered I need regular time away from work and people, in a place where I know no one will invade. God nurtures me in quiet.

I have found unique ways to nurture the faith God gives me. I plant a large garden each spring, for example. Often I tend my garden early in the morning. The quiet of those hours moves me to prayer. When I neglect to provide such time apart, I lose both my sense of inspiration and my sense of direction. When I do honor my need, and schedule time to practice the presence of God, I return to work and to all the relationships of my life with renewed vision and vigor.

My spiritual formation is also deeply wrapped up with others, especially my relationship with Sherry and the congregation to which we are committed. I guard the times of sharing that Sherry and I schedule into each day. She is often a means of grace to me. I look forward to the presence of God I enjoy during worship with our congregation. Honoring these personal rituals is essential to my spiritual formation. As Chapman suggests, "One must at least pray regularly."

God rarely imposes on us. Jesus, who provides the clearest reflection of God we have, invites people to relate to him. If they refuse, he doesn't nag at them. If we want our souls to be shaped by God, we must make ourselves available to God. We must accept the fact that God wants to give to us much more than God wants anything from us. We must accept the gift of faith and trust that the generosity of God is beyond our wildest believing.

NOTES

Preface

1. For a recent analysis, see William R. Hutchison, ed., *Between the Times: The Travail of the Protestant Establishment in America, 1900—1960* (Cambridge, England: Cambridge University Press, 1989).

Chapter 1

1. Robert N. Bellah, Richard Madsen, William M. Sullivan, Ann Swidler, and Steven M. Tipton, *Habits of the Heart: Individualism and Commitment in American Life* (Berkeley: University of California Press, 1985).

2. Wade Clark Roof and William McKinney, *American Mainline Religion: Its Changing Shape and Future* (New Brunswick, N.J.: Rutgers University Press, 1987).

3. Robert Wuthnow, *The Restructuring of American Religion: Society and Faith Since World War II* (Princeton, N.J.: Princeton University Press, 1988).

4. Will Herberg, *Protestant-Catholic-Jew* (Garden City, N.Y.: Doubleday & Company, 1955).

5. Major works that describe this cultural shift and its results include Dean R. Hoge and David A. Roozen, eds., *Understanding Church Growth and Decline: 1950-1978* (New York: Pilgrim Press, 1979); Roof and McKinney, *American Mainline Religion;* Douglas Alan Walrath, *Frameworks: Patterns of Living and Believing Today* (New York: Pilgrim Press, 1987); Wuthnow, *The Restructuring of American Religion;* William R. Hutchison, ed., *Between the Times: The Travail of the Protestant Establishment in America, 1900-1960* (Cambridge, England: Cambridge University Press, 1989).

6. Peter Schrag, *The End of the American Future* (New York: Simon & Schuster, 1973).

7. This hunger for someone to relate to his or her belief issues has been a major concern of those who do not participate in

any church at least since the 1970s. See Douglas Alan Walrath, "Why Some People May Go Back to Church," and other articles in *Review of Religious Research* 21, no. 4 (Supplement: The Unchurched American: A Second Look, 1980); and *The Unchurched American*, (Princeton, N.J.: Princeton Religion Research Center and the Gallup Organization, 1978).

8. See Roof and McKinney, *American Mainline Religion*, and Hutchison, *Between the Times*.

9. See Hutchinson, *Between the Times;* Walrath, "Why Some People . . . "; and Douglas Alan Walrath, *Options: How to Develop and Share Christian Faith Today* (New York: Pilgrim Press, 1988), ch. 1.

10. Douglas Alan Walrath, *Frameworks: Patterns of Living and Believing Today* (New York: Pilgrim Press, 1987), ch. 5.

11. Sir Arthur Eddington, *New Pathways in Science* (Ann Arbor: University of Michigan Press, 1959), especially ch. 1.

12. See Roof and McKinney, *American Mainline Religion*, especially ch. 5, "The Demography of Religious Change."

13. For a more complete discussion of this point and a summary of the literature in which it is established see my *Frameworks*, ch. 1.

14. Cf. Hosea 11; Luke 15:11-32; Exodus 7-12; Romans 12:19.

15. James Fowler, *Stages of Faith* (San Francisco: Harper & Row, 1981).

16. Matthew 19:13-15. The comments of the writer of the Epistle to Hebrews, encouraging us to move on to maturity of faith are also instructive (Heb. 5:11−6:1).

Chapter 2

1. See especially chapter 1.

2. For a more complete discussion, see Douglas Alan Walrath, *Frameworks: Patterns of Living and Believing Today* (New York: The Pilgrim Press, 1987), ch. 1.

3. W. Grant Hague, M.D., *The Eugenic Marriage: A Personal Guide to the New Science of Better Living and Better Babies* (New York: The Review of Reviews Company, 1916) 2: 156-158.

4. Walrath, *Frameworks*, chs. 1 and 3.

5. George Bernard Shaw, *Saint Joan: A Chronicle Play in Six Scenes and an Epilogue* (Baltimore: Penguin Books, 1951), scene 1.

6. *Central Maine Morning Sentinel*, 21 July 1989, p. 6.

7. See "Here I Was Sitting on the Edge of Eternity, " *Life* 12, no. 10 (September 1989): 28-39. The headline on the cover of the magazine reads, "Finding GOD on Flight 232." Capitalization in the original.

Chapter 3

1. Johannes Pedersen, *Israel: Its Life and Culture* (London: Geoffrey Cumberlege, Oxford University Press, 1926), pp. 182, 198-200. Original text altered to make the language inclusive. For a complete description, see pp. 99-260.

2. Douglas Alan Walrath, *Frameworks: Patterns of Living and Believing Today* (New York: Pilgrim Press, 1987), pp. 28, 29.

3. The book that gave a name to the movement is Nena O'Neill and George O'Neill's *Open Marriage* (New York: Evans, 1972). James Ramsey's *Intimate Friendships* (Englewood Cliffs, N.J.: Prentice-Hall, 1972) offers an excellent description of the participants' perspectives at the height of the movement's popularity. Daniel Yankelovich's *New Rules* (New York: Random House, 1981) describes those who continued to advocate open marriages in the early 1980s.

Chapter 4

1. See Douglas Alan Walrath, *Frameworks: Patterns of Living and Believing Today* (New York: Pilgrim Press, 1987), ch. 2.

2. Winston Churchill, *The Inside of the Cup* (New York: Macmillan Company, 1913).

3. Ibid, pp. 250-252. Italics in the original.

Chapter 5

1. Carl S. Dudley, "Affectional and Directional Orientations to Faith" (Washington, D.C.: Alban Institute, 1982), pp. 3, 4, 7, 9.

2. John Baskin, "The Preacher and the Plumber's Son," *Country Journal* 12, no. 4 (April, 1985): 59, 60. Italics in the original.

3. Dom John Chapman, O.S.B., *Spiritual Letters* (London: Sheed & Ward, New Ark Library ed., 1959), p. 53.

DATE DUE

MAR 2 5 1994		
NOV 7 '97		
OCT 2 1 1999		